INTRODUCING
ISSUES WITH
OPPOSING
VIEWPOINTS®

# Oil

Lauri S. Scherer, *Book Editor*

**GREENHAVEN PRESS**
*A part of Gale, Cengage Learning*

GALE
CENGAGE Learning·

Detroit • New York • San Francisco • New Haven, Conn • Waterville, Maine • London

Elizabeth Des Chenes, *Director, Publishing Solutions*

© 2013 Greenhaven Press, a part of Gale, Cengage Learning

Gale and Greenhaven Press are registered trademarks used herein under license.

*For more information, contact:*
Greenhaven Press
27500 Drake Rd.
Farmington Hills, MI 48331-3535
Or you can visit our Internet site at gale.cengage.com

For product information and technology assistance, contact us at

Gale Customer Support, 1-800-877-4253
For permission to use material from this text or product, submit all requests online at
www.cengage.com/permissions

Further permissions questions can be e-mailed to permissionrequest@cengage.com

Articles in Greenhaven Press anthologies are often edited for length to meet page requirements. In addition, original titles of these works are changed to clearly present the main thesis and to explicitly indicate the author's opinion. Every effort is made to ensure that Greenhaven Press accurately reflects the original intent of the authors. Every effort has been made to trace the owners of copyrighted material.

Cover image © Jaochainoi/Shutterstock.com.

---

**LIBRARY OF CONGRESS CATALOGING-IN-PUBLICATION DATA**

Oil / Lauri S. Scherer, book editor.
    pages cm. -- (Introducing issues with opposing viewpoints)
  Summary: "Introducing Issues with Opposing Viewpoints: Oil: Introducing Issues with Opposing Viewpoints is a series that examines current issues from different viewpoints, set up in a pro/con format"-- Provided by publisher.
  Includes bibliographical references and index.
  ISBN 978-0-7377-6279-2 (hardback)
  1.  Oil wells--United States--Hydraulic fracturing. 2.  Petroleum industry and trade--United States. 3.  Energy consumption--Forecasting.  I. Scherer, Lauri S., editor of compilation.
  TN870.O24 2013
  622'.3382--dc23
                                      2012046004

---

Printed in the United States of America
1 2 3 4 5 6 7 17 16 15 14 13

# Contents

# Foreword

Indulging in a wide spectrum of ideas, beliefs, and perspectives is a critical cornerstone of democracy. After all, it is often debates over differences of opinion, such as whether to legalize abortion, how to treat prisoners, or when to enact the death penalty, that shape our society and drive it forward. Such diversity of thought is frequently regarded as the hallmark of a healthy and civilized culture. As the Reverend Clifford Schutjer of the First Congregational Church in Mansfield, Ohio, declared in a 2001 sermon, "Surrounding oneself with only like-minded people, restricting what we listen to or read only to what we find agreeable is irresponsible. Refusing to entertain doubts once we make up our minds is a subtle but deadly form of arrogance." With this advice in mind, Introducing Issues with Opposing Viewpoints books aim to open readers' minds to the critically divergent views that comprise our world's most important debates.

Introducing Issues with Opposing Viewpoints simplifies for students the enormous and often overwhelming mass of material now available via print and electronic media. Collected in every volume is an array of opinions that captures the essence of a particular controversy or topic. Introducing Issues with Opposing Viewpoints books embody the spirit of nineteenth-century journalist Charles A. Dana's axiom: "Fight for your opinions, but do not believe that they contain the whole truth, or the only truth." Absorbing such contrasting opinions teaches students to analyze the strength of an argument and compare it to its opposition. From this process readers can inform and strengthen their own opinions, or be exposed to new information that will change their minds. Introducing Issues with Opposing Viewpoints is a mosaic of different voices. The authors are statesmen, pundits, academics, journalists, corporations, and ordinary people who have felt compelled to share their experiences and ideas in a public forum. Their words have been collected from newspapers, journals, books, speeches, interviews, and the Internet, the fastest growing body of opinionated material in the world.

Introducing Issues with Opposing Viewpoints shares many of the well-known features of its critically acclaimed parent series, Opposing Viewpoints. The articles are presented in a pro/con format, allowing readers to absorb divergent perspectives side by side. Active reading questions preface each viewpoint, requiring the student to approach the material thoughtfully and carefully. Useful charts, graphs, and cartoons supplement each article. A thorough introduction provides readers with crucial background on an issue. An annotated bibliography points the reader toward articles, books, and websites that contain additional information on the topic. An appendix of organizations to contact contains a wide variety of charities, nonprofit organizations, political groups, and private enterprises that each hold a position on the issue at hand. Finally, a comprehensive index allows readers to locate content quickly and efficiently.

Introducing Issues with Opposing Viewpoints is also significantly different from Opposing Viewpoints. As the series title implies, its presentation will help introduce students to the concept of opposing viewpoints and learn to use this material to aid in critical writing and debate. The series' four-color, accessible format makes the books attractive and inviting to readers of all levels. In addition, each viewpoint has been carefully edited to maximize a reader's understanding of the content. Short but thorough viewpoints capture the essence of an argument. A substantial, thought-provoking essay question placed at the end of each viewpoint asks the student to further investigate the issues raised in the viewpoint, compare and contrast two authors' arguments, or consider how one might go about forming an opinion on the topic at hand. Each viewpoint contains sidebars that include at-a-glance information and handy statistics. A Facts About section located in the back of the book further supplies students with relevant facts and figures.

Following in the tradition of the Opposing Viewpoints series, Greenhaven Press continues to provide readers with invaluable exposure to the controversial issues that shape our world. As John Stuart Mill once wrote: "The only way in which a human being can make some approach to knowing the whole of a subject is by hearing what can be said about it by persons of every variety of opinion and studying all modes in which it can be looked at by every character of mind. No wise man ever acquired his wisdom in any mode but this." It is to this principle that Introducing Issues with Opposing Viewpoints books are dedicated.

# Introduction

After decades of decline, the American oil industry is experiencing a surprising resurgence. Spurred by new technology, better equipment, and rising oil prices (which make extracting oil from tricky places financially worthwhile), the American oil industry was so productive by 2012 that oil seemed once again to be the fuel of the future, even after years of warnings about impending shortages and problems associated with its use.

This new chapter in the story of oil began around the beginning of the twenty-first century, when an oil developer named Jim Henry applied a technique known as fracking to a field of hard limestone in 2003. Fracking involves forcing highly pressurized water and chemicals into rock. The water creates tiny cracks through which oil trapped beneath the surface may escape. Fracking is used to extract natural gas from rock, but oil is more difficult to get via the technique, because its molecules are larger than gas molecules. Despite this difficulty, Henry found that fracking allowed him to extract about three times more oil from the limestone field than did traditional techniques. The main downside of the technique was that it was expensive. Oil did not fetch a high enough price on the world market (at that time, only about $30 per barrel) to make the extraction technique financially worthwhile.

By 2008, however, the situation had vastly changed. A global recession and other complex factors raised the price of oil to a record-breaking $147 per barrel (although prices eventually came down; as of July 2012 they were still relatively high, at about $85 per barrel). With producers able to recoup the money they spent on the fracking process, the industry took off. New oil fields were opened in North Dakota, Kansas, Wyoming, Colorado, Texas, and even Ohio. Together, these yielded nearly an additional million barrels of oil per day (bpd). In 2008, for example, the United States produced about 4.95 million bpd; by 2012 it was up to approximately 5.7 million bpd. Production was so great that the US Department of Energy predicted that by 2020 the United States might produce as much as 7 million bpd, while other experts predicted 10 million bpd. Should this be the case, the United States could theoretically produce as much per day as oil giant Saudi Arabia (which produced around 10 million bpd in May 2012).

Fracking was not the only technique that led to America's oil boom—advances in technology made it easier to drill for oil deep in the ocean, too. Rigs in the Gulf of Mexico, for example, now use complex imaging software to locate underwater oil fields. Advanced seismic technology further helps them to pinpoint an underwater oil field's location and size. It also indicates whether oil is hidden under layers of salt or other substances that require specialized drilling. Drilling equipment, too, has improved: Higher-quality metals can better withstand the kinds of temperature and pressure extremes found in very deep water. As a result, in 2012 the US Energy Information Administration (EIA) estimated that the Gulf of Mexico was producing about 1.23 million bpd and accounted for more than 20 percent of US oil production (even despite regulations put in place after the 2010 *Deepwater Horizon* oil spill, which temporarily halted and then scaled back deepwater drilling operations in the gulf).

The net result of all of these developments is that the United States is, for the first time in decades, awash in oil from its own territory. "We're having a revolution," declares G. Steven Farris of Apache Corporation, an oil producer in West Texas. "And we're just scratching the surface."[1] *New York Times* reporters Clifford Krauss and Eric Lipton report that an influx of domestically produced oil has far-reaching implications for many aspects of American culture. "Taken together," they write, "the increasing production and declining consumption have unexpectedly brought the United States markedly closer to a goal that has tantalized presidents since Richard Nixon: independence from foreign energy sources, a milestone that could reconfigure American foreign policy, the economy and more."[2]

But even if the American oil boom could solve problems posed by foreign oil dependence and a dwindling oil supply, other problems associated with oil use remain. For example, concerns remain that burning oil contributes to climate change and other environmental devastation, no matter how cheap it becomes or how much is domestically produced. Fracking particularly takes a toll on the environment: residents near the new oil towns in Wyoming, North Dakota, and elsewhere complain their air and water quality have declined as a result of exploration operations. Others fear large swaths of valuable habitat will be ruined by extracting oil from the ground. Furthermore, extending the era of oil will actually make environmental problems worse in the long run, according to those who argue that oil use contributes to climate change and oil should thus be abandoned completely as an energy source. "We need to start reducing emissions significantly, not create new ways to increase them"[3] suggests James Hansen of NASA's Goddard Institute for Space Studies.

America's surprising new identity as a petrostate and how this status will affect the economy, the environment, and civilization are among the many issues explored in *Introducing Issues with Opposing Viewpoints: Oil.* Readers will also consider thoughtful arguments about whether oil is a finite or renewable resource, whether it has implications for national security, whether there will ever be a post-oil era, and what alternative energy sources might efficiently replace oil. Critical reading comprehension questions and thought-provoking essay prompts further encourage students to develop their own opinions on this enduring and multifaceted topic.

## Notes
1. Quoted in Clifford Krauss and Eric Lipton, "U.S. Inches Toward Goal of Energy Independence," *New York Times*, March 22, 2012. www.nytimes.com/2012/03/23/business/energy-environment/inching-toward-energy-independence-in-america.html?pagewanted=all.
2. Krauss and Lipton, "U.S. Inches Toward Goal of Energy Independence."
3. James Hansen, "Game Over for the Climate," *New York Times*, May 9, 2012. www.nytimes.com/2012/05/10/opinion/game-over-for-the-climate.html.

# Chapter 1

# Is Oil Running Out?

*As the world uses more oil it is becoming increasingly difficult to cheaply extract the earth's remaining oil deposits.*

**Viewpoint**

**1**

# Oil Is a Finite Resource

### David Ingles and Richard Denniss

*"The time for the world to worry about peak oil is now, while there is a window of opportunity to do something about it."*

In the following viewpoint David Ingles and Richard Denniss argue it is inevitable that the world will run out of oil. They explain that oil is a finite resource, meaning there is a limited amount of it on earth. They discuss a commonly held point of view, which is that oil is created by complex geological processes that take millions of years to complete. The effect is that the oil burned today will not be replenished within a useful time frame. Each year, the authors warn, humans use more oil than they find, which is another indicator that they will eventually run out of oil if they keep consuming it at current rates. The authors admit that new technologies might make it possible to extract new oil from difficult or expensive places, but they warn that the environmental costs of doing so make that oil unreasonable to use. They conclude that the world is running out of oil and humans should find a replacement energy source as soon as possible. Ingles and Denniss are analysts with the Australia Institute, a think tank and policy organization based in Canberra, Australia.

David Ingles and Richard Denniss, "Running on Empty? The Peak Oil Debate," *The Australia Institute*, vol. 16, September 2010, pp. 2–5. Copyright © 2010 by The Australia Institute. All rights reserved. Reproduced by permission.

**AS YOU READ, CONSIDER THE FOLLOWING QUESTIONS:**
1. According to the authors, how many gigabarrels of oil were found each year between 2002 and 2007? How many gigabarrels of oil were used per year during that time?
2. Who is M. King Hubbert, and how does he factor into the authors' argument?
3. How might climate change impact potential solutions to peak oil, according to the authors?

L ike climate change, the possibility of peak oil poses an uncomfortable challenge to citizens and governments alike in the 21st century. 'Peak oil' is the term used to describe the point in time at which the worldwide production of crude oil extraction will be maximised. But while it is inevitable that production will peak at some point, it is uncertain when that point will be reached.

## We Use More Oil than We Find

Peak oil concerns exploded during the rapid escalation of oil prices prior to the 2007 global financial crisis (GFC), and resurfaced recently when oil prices appeared to resume their upward trend. These concerns have been underscored by official bodies such as the International Energy Agency (IEA) warning of a possible 'supply crunch' brought about by a lack of new investment following the GFC.

World oil field discoveries (as distinct from the amount of oil extracted) peaked in the 1960s at around 55 Gigabarrels (Gb) a year, but fewer than 10 Gb a year have been discovered between 2002 and 2007. Current demand is 31 Gb a year. According to official estimates, around 40 to 75 years of supply remains at existing usage rates but much fewer if demand continues to grow. Although usage has more or less stabilised in developed western countries, the rapid economic growth of populous nations such as China and India is creating significant upward pressure on the demand for oil products.

## Not a Matter of "If" but "When"

There is not much disagreement about the concept of peak oil, but there is fierce debate about how near the world is to the peak and what, if anything, should be done about it. In fact, a substantial amount of oil remains in the earth and peak oil doomsayers have often been proved wrong in the past. But this is not a reason for complacency. Oil is a precious resource; there is a finite supply in the earth and there is no reason at all to use it wastefully. Moreover, as the IEA has argued, the world is currently embarked on a fossil-fuel future that is patently unsustainable from an environmental perspective, quite apart from the fact that rates of extraction will exhaust fossil-fuel resources far too quickly, thus ignoring the needs of future generations. . . .

*World oil discovery peaked in the 1960s at nearly 55 gigabarrels a year, but by 2007, fewer than 10 gigabarrels a year were being discovered.*

Peak oil is the proposition that there is a finite supply of oil in the earth and, at some point, it will no longer be possible to increase production in response to rising demand. Indeed, the supply of oil will plateau and begin to fall.

Peak-oil scares have come and gone as the price of oil has waxed and waned over the past three decades. Currently, fears are in abeyance as motorists have become accustomed to pump prices at around $1.30 a litre [about $5.00 per gallon], although this is still considerably higher than was the case several years ago. But prices are on a long-term upward trend and seem likely to spike again when the world economy regains some strength following the GFC.

While demand for oil appears to have stabilised in the developed world, the rapid growth of countries like India and China will create a significant rising demand. This paper argues that the time for the world to worry about peak oil is now, while there is a window of opportunity to do something about it. It does not make economic or social sense to delay action until prices are already rising sharply.

## The Theory of Peak Oil

World oil production is the sum total of the production of individual countries, but the oil supply of many countries, including Australia, is now beginning to exhibit peaking qualities or is already assumed to be past its peak. The concept of peak oil is primarily associated with the US geologist M King Hubbert ('Hubbert's peak'), who in the 1950s predicted that US oil production would peak in about 1970, a prediction borne out by events. Hubbert's mathematical model and its variants have described with reasonable accuracy the peak and decline of production from oil wells, fields, regions and countries. However, his estimates for the world peak, 1995–2000, were clearly early and well below actual production. . . .

The idea that oil is a finite resource and production will peak at some point is not disputed but predictions about the timing of the

# When Will the Oil Run Out?

As world consumption increases, known supplies of fossil fuels are projected to decline. Some organizations have predicted that all of the oil will be gone by the end of the twenty-first century.

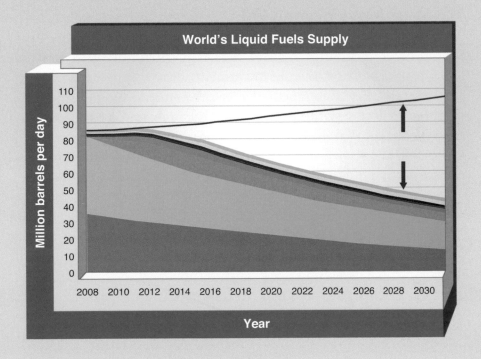

**World's Liquid Fuels Supply**

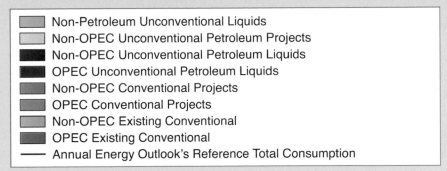

- Non-Petroleum Unconventional Liquids
- Non-OPEC Unconventional Petroleum Projects
- Non-OPEC Unconventional Petroleum Liquids
- OPEC Unconventional Petroleum Liquids
- Non-OPEC Conventional Projects
- OPEC Conventional Projects
- Non-OPEC Existing Conventional
- OPEC Existing Conventional
- Annual Energy Outlook's Reference Total Consumption

Note: OPEC stands for the Organization of the Petroleum Exporting Countries.

Taken from: World's Liquid Fuels Supply, *Annual Energy Outlook*, Energy Information Administration, 2009, p. 8.

peak attract controversy. Some people believe that it is imminent, or indeed already here, while others believe that new discoveries, higher prices and technological innovation will place the peak far in the future. There is also a view held by some that the peak simply does not matter because alternatives to oil will gradually assume more significance as the price makes it economic to produce them.

## We Must Move Beyond Oil

The principal contention concerning peak oil is what, if anything, should be done about it. Laissez-faire economists take the view that rising oil prices will stimulate investments in new exploration, energy efficiency and the development of alternatives such as biofuels and these, over time, will automatically take care of the problem. In contrast, many experts consider that the transition to a post-oil economy will be incredibly disruptive if not handled well, with the possibility of rolling recessions when central banks react to price spikes by slowing economies.

While peak oil and climate change are clearly separate problems, there is a high degree of overlap in the potential solutions. In addition, climate change may limit the ways in which the world is able to adapt to peak oil by ruling out some, or even many, unconventional oil resources on the basis of the greenhouse gas emissions involved in their extraction. The climate-change issue is also relevant in that some peak-oil adaptations, for example energy conservation, will also help ameliorate climate change. Like climate change, peak oil requires a move away from the historic reliance on fossil fuels into a 'post carbon' economy.

## EVALUATING THE AUTHOR'S ARGUMENTS:

David Ingles and Richard Denniss argue that the point at which to move away from oil is now, while there is still time to invest in and transition to alternative energy systems. How do you think each of the authors in this chapter would respond to this claim? For each author, write one to two sentences stating their probable position. Then state your opinion—do you agree with them? Why or why not?

# Oil Is a Renewable Resource

**Greg Lewis**

*"Oil is in fact a renewable resource that is being constantly created deep under the earth's surface."*

In the following viewpoint Greg Lewis suggests that oil may not be a finite resource, as is commonly believed. Conventional theories hold oil to be created by geological and biological processes that take place over millions of years. But Lewis argues this is not the case—he presents new evidence that suggests oil is continually produced by microscopic organisms that interact with hydrocarbons deep below the earth's surface. Lewis is convinced that oil is a replenishable resource that will never run out. Given this, he says, energy policy based on the notion that oil is finite is simply not true: There is no need to transition to other sources of energy, especially when doing so would harm the economy. The author hopes Americans will consider that oil is replenishable, renewable, and available forever to them as an energy source and recognize the important economic, environmental, and political ramifications this idea has. Lewis is a writer for *American Thinker*, a publication that considers a wide variety of current events and social issues from a critical, often conservative, perspective.

**AS YOU READ, CONSIDER THE FOLLOWING QUESTIONS:**
  1. Who is Thomas Gold and what bearing does he have on the author's argument?
  2. What is Eugene Island and how does it factor into Lewis's argument?
  3. In Lewis's opinion, what mass deceit invites what mass enslavement?

P resident Barack Obama and his green energy confederates are determined to scare the public about a declining supply of "fossil fuels." If we accept the idea that oil is produced by the conversion of organic matter—from plants to dinosaurs—under extreme pressure, we must also accept the idea that there is a limited supply of oil and that we've got to do everything we can to find a replacement for fossil fuels before we run out.

## What If Oil Is a Renewable Resource?

The evidence is mounting that not only do we have more than a century's worth of recoverable oil in the United States alone (even if there is a limit to the earth's oil supply), but that we also actually have a limitless supply of Texas tea [oil] because oil is in fact a renewable resource that is being constantly created deep under the earth's surface and which rises upward, where microscopic organisms that thrive in the intense pressure and heat miles below us interact with and alter it.

In other words, we have an unending supply of oil, some of which is constantly migrating upward from the depths at which it is created to refill existing oil deposits, and much more of which remains far below the surface. This oil can be recovered using existing technology.

## The Earth Is Constantly Making New Oil

Scientist Thomas Gold presents the decades-old theory of "abiotic" oil-creation, which supports these facts, in his book, *The Deep Hot Biosphere.* In it he explains that the idea of the "biotic" creation of "fossil fuels"—that decaying organic matter is compressed into oil— is incorrect. In fact, the earth is constantly producing new oil very deep below its surface, and in some cases the oil flows up to replenish existing oil fields thought to be exhausted. In simple terms, the microscopic organisms mentioned above interact with the hydrocarbons, altering them and leaving their footprint, thus disproving the notion that oil is a "fossil fuel."

Here's an example of how the process plays out:

Eugene Island is an underwater mountain located about 80 miles off the coast of Louisiana in the Gulf of Mexico. In 1973 oil was struck and off-shore platform Eugene 330 erected. The field began production at 15,000 barrels a day, then gradually fell off, as is normal, to 4,000 barrels a day in 1989. Then came the surprise; it reversed itself and increased production to 13,000 barrels a day. Probable reserves have been increased to 400 million barrels from 60 million. The field appears to be filling from below and the crude coming up today is from a geological age different from the original crude, which leads to the speculation that the world has limitless supplies of petroleum.

*This oil refinery is in Russia. Russia developed technology in the 1970s to test the theory of refilling oil fields. Its success allowed Russian oil production to increase.*

## "The Field Appears to Be Filling"

The theory of what Gold calls the deep hot biosphere was explored more fully in Stalinist Russia in the 1940s when the Russian dictator demanded that his scientists find a way to increase Soviet oil production. As they explored the idea that oil and other hydrocarbons are constantly being generated deep beneath the earth's surface, Russian technology was developed in the 1970s to test the theory by drilling as deep as 40,000 feet into the earth. As a result, Russia was the first nation to begin to understand and exploit these renewable oil reserves, and today their oil industry is thriving.

The political implications for Barack Obama and the radical environmentalist base he panders to with his corrupt "renewable" energy policy are profound. First, as we've seen, the president continually misrepresents the amount of recoverable oil available to us. His assertion that we have "only two percent of the world's oil reserves" available to us is simply a lie. . . . We're awash in oil reserves, and it's up to our political candidates to expose Obama's baseless fabrications about our energy reserves.

## The Green Agenda Is Based on a Lie

Beyond that, most Americans have digested the fact that the entire environmentalist rationale for pursuing "green energy" technology is built on fabricated global warming—recently renamed "climate change"—science. To continue to pursue a path based on such deceit—that the earth is warming and we must convert to "renewable" energy sources ASAP—is to invite enslavement to an economy dominated by energy produced by Obama's political cronies and controlled, ultimately, by a central government. It's also to ignore the fact that the earth itself is a producer of virtually limitless supplies of the very renewable energy on which the infrastructure of modern civilization is built.

The public . . . is ready for a message that defends oil as the fuel of the future and is buttressed by growing scientific evidence. This means that there's no need for us to look beyond our shores—our "offshores," to be precise—to discover where our oil is coming from. It's bubbling up constantly from miles below the surface of the earth, and it's not about to run out.

## EVALUATING THE AUTHOR'S ARGUMENTS:

That oil is a finite resource is typically accepted as fact, even among those who disagree that oil should be abandoned as an energy source. Yet Greg Lewis presents information that challenges this conventional wisdom. If he is correct and oil is in fact a renewable resource, how would this change your opinion of oil as an energy source? Are there still reasons to abandon it? Would it comfort you to think of oil as renewable? Reflect on this game-changing suggestion offered by Lewis.

# When Oil Runs Out, Society Will Break Down

## Steve Hallett and John Wright

*"To picture a world suddenly without oil [is to picture] a complete and rapid breakdown of society, leading to desperation, lawlessness, wars and untold suffering."*

In the following viewpoint Steve Hallett and John Wright imagine what the world would be like without oil. Transportation would grind to a halt, they say. Because cities and towns have been designed for vehicle use, people would be stranded, cut off from their families, friends, workplaces, and shops. Their homes would be plunged into darkness, and the devices and appliances on which they depend to survive would be rendered useless. They would not have easy access to food, which is delivered and refrigerated using oil. People also would not be able to rely on most modern products, medicines, tools, and other essentials that are made from oil. A world without oil is a world without everything, they conclude. To avoid the inevitable chaos that will come when oil runs out, Hallett and Wright urge society to switch to a different energy source as soon as possible—before catastrophe strikes.

Hallett is an associate professor of botany at Purdue University. Wright is the Latin America news editor for *Energy News Today*. Together they wrote the book *Life Without Oil: Why We Must Shift to a New Energy Future*.

**AS YOU READ, CONSIDER THE FOLLOWING QUESTIONS:**
1. What does the term *price-gouging* mean in the context of the viewpoint?
2. Name at least five products the authors say are made from oil.
3. In what ways would a sudden disappearance of oil affect the food supply, according to the authors?

D ismantle the oil rigs and stack them in a pile. Radio the tankers and order them back to port. Pull out the drills and cement up the wells. (A year after the BP spill in the Gulf of Mexico,[1] let's hope we've learned how to do *that*, at least.) Tow the platforms back to shore. Plug up the pipelines. And lock up the Strategic Petroleum Reserve while you're at it—it has only about a month or so worth of oil in it, anyway.

What would happen next? How would we live in a world without oil?

## When the Needles Point to "E"

First, there's transportation. With the overwhelming majority of the oil we produce and import devoted to powering our cars, motorcycles, trucks, trains and planes, the impact on getting around would be most dramatic. Price-gouging would begin right away, and long lines would form at gas stations. The lines wouldn't last, though, because the gasoline would soon be gone. A strategic reserve of finished petroleum products—gasoline, diesel and aviation fuel—has often been suggested but never created. Within a month, every fuel tank would be dry, all our gauge needles would point to "E," and the roads, rails and skies would be virtually empty.

How far is it to the nearest grocery store? How long does it take to walk—or bike, or skate—to work? Finally confronting our dependence

1. The spill released about 4.9 million barrels of oil into the Gulf of Mexico in 2010.

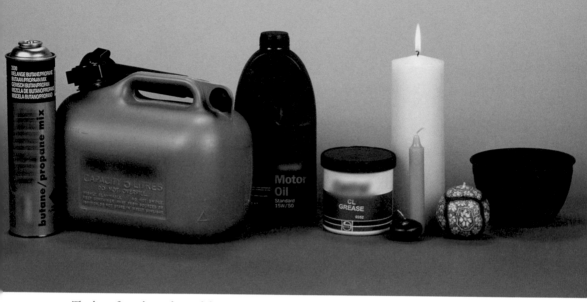

*The list of products derived from oil is almost endless. It includes plastics, medicines, paints, ballpoint pens, Barbie dolls, golf balls, and more.*

on motor vehicles, we'd reach for whatever solutions we could find. Soon, we'd all be looking for an electric car (but there are precious few of those for sale) or converting our vehicles to run on natural gas. But we'd be waiting for some time to secure adequate natural gas supplies, establish delivery infrastructure and switch over our cars.

## The Price of Enslavement

Our enslavement to black gold goes much further than the problem of getting from Point A to Point B. We also need to keep the lights on. And this would be possible, for the first month or so, because only 1 percent of America's electricity is generated from oil—coal carries the largest burden, along with natural gas, nuclear and hydroelectric power.

But brownouts and blackouts would soon begin. Sure, our electricity is generated mostly from coal, but how would the coal be extracted without those diesel-guzzling yellow trucks? How would it be hauled to the power plants? (Remember, our trains all run on diesel, too). Heating and cooling our homes would suddenly get a lot more complicated, and our televisions and laptops would be just a few more weeks away from shutting off forever.

## A World Without Oil Is a World Without Everything

Forget even trying to get to work anymore; we now have another set of problems to solve, especially if it's winter and our houses are getting cold. Can we quickly put together some solar panels and batteries? A wind turbine? What do we have growing in the back yard that can burn? Environmentalists have been nudging us to insulate our homes and generate electricity from renewable resources for a while now; this might be the time to start paying attention.

It gets much worse still, of course, because a world without oil would quickly become a world without all of the products made from petroleum that we have come to know, love and depend upon. The list of essentials that we'd soon be doing without is prodigious: virtually all plastics, paints, medicines, hospital machines that go "bleep," Barbie dolls, ballpoint pens, breast implants, golf balls. . . .

Eating would get tougher, too. If no one can truck in fresh veggies from across the country, we might be inclined to go back to basics and grow our own food. Local farmers would become a necessity, not just people who sell us honey at the street fair. That said, make sure to keep the food coming, fresh and fast, because it's going to be awfully difficult to refrigerate. Fishing might work, so you'd need to get a new rod while supplies last. Alas, most of them are made of plastic. Then again, so is fishing line.

> **FAST FACT**
>
> A 2007 poll taken by Metabolix found that 72 percent of Americans do not realize that plastic products (such as bags, toothbrushes, toys, bottles, and other items) are derived from oil.

## A Complete and Rapid Breakdown of Society

It's an interesting thought experiment to picture a world suddenly without oil. Taken to its logical conclusion, it encompasses so much more: a complete and rapid breakdown of society, leading to desperation,

# The Last Century of Oil?

Some sources predict that by the end of the century, global oil production will significantly decline. How society might handle such an event remains to be seen.

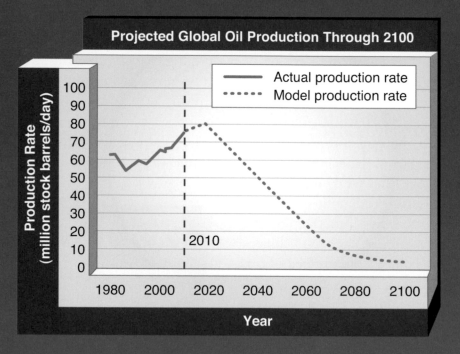

**Projected Global Oil Production Through 2100**

Production Rate (million stock barrels/day)

— Actual production rate

····· Model production rate

Year

Taken from: Ibrahim Sami Nashawi, Adel Malallah, and Mohammed al-Bisharah. "Forecasting World Crude Oil Production Using Multicyclic Hubbert Model." Kuwait University, March 2010. http://pubs.asc.org/doi/abs/10.10 21/ef901240p.

lawlessness, wars and untold suffering. The scenario is unreal, of course, because we could never shut off our oil supply in a day, and in any case, there are trillions of barrels of the stuff still in the ground, right?

Yet, in a simpler sense, it's not so unrealistic, because even if it will happen more gradually than laid out here, we will indeed run out of oil. Output has already peaked in the majority of countries and has been declining in the United States since 1971. A handful of countries are still increasing production, but not enough to offset even bigger declines elsewhere. There is lots of oil still in the ground (we've used about half of the planet's generous endowment), but while the end of oil may be many decades away, the beginning of the end is now.

It's not just at the drip of the final drop that the oil crisis begins. It is when production stagnates and begins its inexorable fall. That perilous moment, alas, is now. Our oil supplies are about to begin to fail us. As oil becomes more scarce, we have to get serious about finding new solutions to power our world.

We have time to plan—but not that much time. And so far, we've done very little to prepare for a world without oil.

## EVALUATING THE AUTHOR'S ARGUMENTS:

Steve Hallett and John Wright conjure up apocalyptic visions of a world plunged suddenly into chaos. How do you think each of the authors represented in this chapter would respond to their vision? Write one to two sentences on what you think each author's probable response would be. Then state your own opinion. Is it useful to look ahead to a world without oil? Why or why not?

# The World Will Never Have to Make Do Without Oil

## Dieter Helm

"*The oil Armageddon is unlikely to be emerging.*"

Dieter Helm is a professor of energy policy at the University of Oxford and the author of *The Carbon Crunch*. In the following viewpoint he says the world will never have to make do without oil—so there is no point imagining doomsday scenarios about a world plunged into chaos as a result of a sudden oil shortage. He says advances in technology are yielding more oil all the time and contributing to systems that burn oil more efficiently and cleanly. It makes no sense to waste money on low-impact oil alternatives that do not work as well, he says. In his opinion, people who warn about a chaotic oil-free world are alarmists; they trade in hype without understanding facts. Helm concludes it is silly to waste time pondering apocalyptic scenarios and worrying about an era that is unlikely ever to come to pass.

**AS YOU READ, CONSIDER THE FOLLOWING QUESTIONS:**
1. How much will offshore wind programs cost Britain by 2020, according to the author?
2. What is contained beneath the ice in the Arctic, and how does it factor into the author's argument?
3. What important energy source does the author say is still in its infancy?

P eak oil—the idea that we have passed or are about to pass the physical peak of oil production—is again in fashion. It has been lent impetus by events in the Middle East and North Africa. Predictions abound of imminent price shocks, $200-a-barrel oil, and an oil-induced Armageddon. We have been here before: it is all very reminiscent of the reactions to the Iranian revolution and the oil price shock in 1979 when oil prices hit $39 a barrel (about $130 in current money).

## Oil Alarmism Has Serious Consequences

Belief in this coming Armageddon naturally underpins the case for going green, and in particular for placing overwhelming emphasis on renewables and energy efficiency measures. Current extremely expensive offshore wind programmes (amounting to over £100bn [100 billion British pounds] in Britain before 2020) become economic, advocates of this argument say, because the price of the alternative is going to be so high. Energy efficiency becomes more attractive at high oil prices, the argument goes, and hence the demand for energy will fall (at least for the domestic market) thereby offsetting the costs of renewables. Thus the strategy pays for itself.

From an environmental perspective it all looks too good to be true—and it is. Almost all that could be wrong with this argument is wrong—there is no obvious peak in oil production; what matters for electricity is gas (and coal), not oil; and there are few reasons to think that energy demand is likely to fall. Renewables will increase retail prices a lot. The one thing that remains is that offshore wind is about the most expensive means to achieving limited carbon reductions.

## There Is Plenty of Oil

Let's start with the notion of peak oil. It is true that current (conventional) oil reserves are concentrated in the Middle East. There is an Opec [Organization of the Petroleum Exporting Countries] premium in the oil price, and right now there is clearly a Libyan premium too, and perhaps more shocks to come. But there is still a lot of conventional oil. Iraq has yet to fully enter the market. It plans to produce more extra oil by 2020 than Saudi Arabia's entire production today. Saudi has lots of "swing production"—the capacity to produce more to compensate for shortfalls elsewhere. Africa is now a much more important part of the arithmetic. Then there is Brazil, and offshore fields in the US. Add in the enormous reserves in the Arctic as the ice melts, and Russia's immense reserves, and a rather different picture emerges. Finally, production assumptions are based upon depletion rates typically below 50 per cent of a field's reserves: add in a bit of technical progress and the story changes substantially.

> **FAST FACT**
>
> Michael Lynch of the Center for International Studies at the Massachusetts Institute of Technology reports that in the early twentieth century, only 10 percent of the planet's known oil was considered recoverable; in the twenty-first century, more than 35 percent is considered recoverable.

Even were the worst fears of peak oil advocates to emerge, the consequences for electricity (and renewables) are far from obvious. The fossil fuel of choice for electricity generation is gas, not oil, and gas is super-abundant. The coming of shale gas has doubled the world's gas reserves in a couple of years, the US has become an exporter and its shale gas production costs are such that it is competing on cost with natural gas. Shale gas has its problems, but the fact is that the reserves are very large and widely distributed—in the US, China, Europe, Russia, the Middle East and elsewhere. In Australia even coal-bed methane is being liquefied and exported to China.

This transformation is no accident: much more research and development (R&D) has been applied to fossil fuels than renewables. In the shale gas case, it is the combination of IT [information technology]

# Plenty of Oil for the Future

Oil reserves and production grow each year, leading some to believe there will be plenty available well into the future.

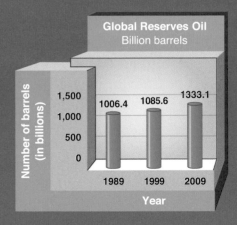

**Global Reserves Oil**
Billion barrels

Number of barrels (in billions)

1,500
1,000
500
0

1006.4 (1989)  1085.6 (1999)  1333.1 (2009)

Year

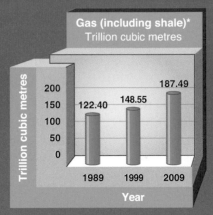

**Gas (including shale)\***
Trillion cubic metres

Trillion cubic metres

200
150
100
50
0

122.40 (1989)  148.55 (1999)  187.49 (2009)

Year

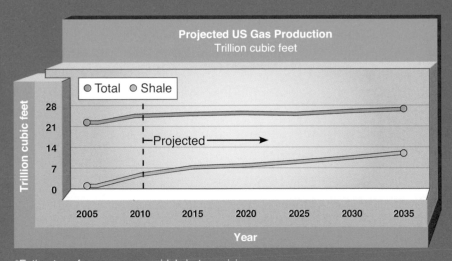

**Projected US Gas Production**
Trillion cubic feet

Trillion cubic feet

● Total  ● Shale

28
21
14
7
0

←Projected→

2005  2010  2015  2020  2025  2030  2035

Year

*Estimates of reserves vary widely but are rising.

Taken from: BP, IEA, Prospect Research.

advances in seismic surveying, horizontal drilling and techniques for fracturing the shale rock to release the gas. The result is that, for policy purposes, we can assume that the supply of gas is almost infinite, and there are large-scale deposits of shale oil, coal and tar sands. The earth's crust is riddled with carbon fuels. Contrary to the peak oilers, there is no physical shortage of fossil fuels—and that's the real problem. . . .

## Technology Will Yield More Oil and Make It Cleaner

So the oil Armageddon is unlikely to be emerging, despite short-term volatility. But the coming of shale gas represents much more. As I have said, gas is the fuel of choice for electricity generation, and electricity is the power of choice for final use. Electricity is gradually taking over. To date it's been supported by coal, and the growing share of coal in world primary fuel sources is the main explanation for the growth of carbon emissions—on which (as a result) Kyoto [the Kyoto Protocol, an agreement aimed at fighting climate change] has made almost no impact.

The hegemony of electricity is arguably still in its infancy. Smart grids and smart meters are a technical revolution waiting to happen. Electric cars transform the storage of electricity (it's in the batteries) and increase electricity demand—and lower demand for oil (because transport has been the main source of growth in demand for oil). Once electric cars get a grip, oil is of much less relevance—gas, in effect, displaces oil via electricity. Peak oilers assume not only that oil is in fixed supply, but that it is not interchangeable with other fossil fuels. They are just wrong. In due course we might even end up leaving a lot of the oil in the ground.

## Oil Alternatives Are Expensive and Do Not Solve Problems

The implications for climate change policy are profound. On the one hand, cheap and abundant fossil fuels make renewables expensive and deter investments in energy efficiency. Demand grows. On the other hand, coal is twice as bad from a carbon perspective as gas. If gas displaces coal (especially in China, India and the US) really big inroads could be made quickly into carbon emissions. Add in some significant nuclear investments, and there is the making of an intermediary (and very cheap) transition to a lower carbon world.

*New technologies have been developed to extract natural gas from shale, a type of soft, layered rock. The technologies have allowed access to an almost unlimited supply of gas for energy use.*

Further out, technical change takes over. There has probably never been a time when there is more R&D in energy technologies. The range of ideas and concepts is enormous. There is no shortage of energy supply: the sun comes up every day. The task is to harness the opportunities. It is not to reduce the demand for energy which has the power to transform the lives of billions. Energy efficiency (an obvious good thing) is not the same as energy demand reduction (not necessarily a good thing). No amount of fitting of draft-excluders, double glazing or wall insulation will have much impact on global warming—what matters is initially lower carbon ways of getting the energy (that is, gas) and then low carbon ways (through R&D and new technology).

In the short run, the impact of low carbon technology "winners" governments have (foolishly) picked is going to be tough. All those offshore windmills are going to remain very expensive and politicians who have rushed to say otherwise (in part, on the basis of peak oil) have not helped. Telling people something is going to be economic when it is unlikely to be is hardly the way to get carbon credibility. Better to face down the lobbyists and to tell the truth: offshore wind is very expensive and likely to remain so.

Politicians can of course carry on with this deception for as long as not much offshore wind is built. But as the rush in the next nine years towards perhaps as much as 30 gigawatts gets underway to meet the EU [European Union] 2020 target, the impact on the bills will start to show. Here there are two conditions which need to be met: that customers can actually pay; and that they are willing to vote for politicians who will force them to pay. By around 2016, both of these conditions will be put to the test.

## Oil Alarmism Is Nonsense

Fortunately there is a better way forward. The first step is to recognise that peak oil alarmism is nonsense. Oil is not likely to run out any time soon and in any event it is fungible—replaceable—with gas. The second step is to recognize the impact of the shale gas revolution—and the implications for the wider production of carbon based fuels. The problem is there is too much fossil fuel, not too little—and if we burn it all we will fry. This is the real threat. The third step is to be realistic with the politics. Truth telling comes hard, but it is a much better way of addressing the politics of climate change than claiming that the transition to a low carbon economy can be relatively painless.

## EVALUATING THE AUTHOR'S ARGUMENTS:

Dieter Helm and the authors of the previous viewpoint, Steve Hallett and John Wright, disagree on whether it is useful to imagine a world without oil. Helm considers this alarmist; Hallett and Wright consider this pragmatic and illuminating. What do you think? Are people who warn about a world without oil alarmist, or are they thoughtfully considering a likely future? Explain your reasoning.

# Chapter 2

# What Problems Come with Oil Use?

The April 21, 2010, Deepwater Horizon *oil rig explosion in the Gulf of Mexico and the subsequent environmental disaster illustrated the high environmental risks involved with using oil.*

## Viewpoint

## 1

# Oil Is a Very Problematic Resource

### Susan Lyon, Rebecca Lefton, and Daniel J. Weiss

*"One in five barrels of U.S. oil come from countries that the State Department considers to be 'dangerous or unstable.'"*

In the following viewpoint Susan Lyon, Rebecca Lefton, and Daniel J. Weiss detail the ways in which oil use causes economic, political, and environmental problems. They explain that when countries like China and India consume more and more oil, there is less of it to go around. As a result, China and India are forced to make energy deals with unstable, dangerous, but oil-rich nations. This threatens global security by sending billions of dollars to dangerous dictatorships and warring countries. Because it is increasingly scarce, oil is also increasingly expensive—the authors say this hurts families, businesses, and economies all over the world. When countries spend a lot of money on oil, they do not have funds to invest in progressive energy sources and other productive ventures. Finally, oil exploration and extraction hurt the environment and cause tragedy, such as the April 2010 explosion of the *Deepwater Horizon*, which killed eleven people and spilled millions of barrels of oil into the Gulf of Mexico. For all of these reasons, the authors conclude, oil is rife with problems and should be replaced with a less problematic energy source. Lyon, Lefton, and Weiss work for the Center for American Progress, a think tank that makes policy recommendations on a wide variety of topics, including energy.

## AS YOU READ, CONSIDER THE FOLLOWING QUESTIONS:
1. How many barrels of US oil come from dangerous or unstable countries, according to the authors?
2. With which unstable, developing nations is India pursuing energy deals, according to the authors?
3. In what way do gas price increases affect American families, according to the authors?

The national security risks that stem from the United States' heavy reliance on foreign oil are well documented. One in five barrels of U.S. oil come from countries that the State Department considers to be "dangerous or unstable." And the cost of this oil will rise as global demand increases. These high prices benefit all petro-states regardless of whether the United States is buying from them or not. The United States doesn't buy Iranian oil, for example, but a $1 increase in oil prices provides an additional $1.5 billion to the Iranian government annually.

The International Energy Agency [IEA] notes that the United States also remains vulnerable to a Middle East oil disruption: "U.S. dependence on the long-haul Middle East has fallen sharply . . . [but] since oil is a global market, the relevant measure for that vulnerability is not U.S. dependence, but world dependence on Middle East oil—and that has not shrunk."

Our allies cannot fill this supply gap. Canada and Mexico are our largest importers. But a majority of Canadian oil comes from tar sands—a dirty crude oil that can cause as much as five times more greenhouse gas pollution to produce compared to conventional oil. And Mexico's primary oil sources will be depleted by 2019.

Global oil demand—led by the United States and followed by China, Japan, and India—will dramatically increase over the next two decades. China has made oil deals around the world over the past few years that can deliver a supply of more than 7.8 billion barrels of oil to the country over the next several years. The United States must meanwhile prepare for a coming oil price crunch caused by increasing global demand and slowing global production. The safest, cheapest, and fastest path to energy security is to implement oil savings measures . . . to reduce dependence on foreign oil and protect our pocketbooks. . . .

## China and India Will Support Dangerous Nations

Chinese leaders want to secure future oil supplies to meet [their] anticipated demand. China's partially government-owned national oil companies are pursuing oil deals abroad. They have made exploration and production deals in Iran, Sudan, and Venezuela, as well as with other "energy-rich problem states," throughout the last decade.

*China's rapidly increasing need for oil has led the country to make deals to import more than 7.8 billion barrels of oil over the next few years, which will drive up the price of energy.*

And a survey of China's most recent overseas oil deals finds that these contracts hold the combined potential to deliver more than 7.8 billion barrels of oil to China.

This heavy investment can funnel money to unstable or dangerous regimes. China has been the largest foreign investor in Sudanese oil fields and indirectly funded governments in Venezuela, Myanmar, and Iran. China also provides economic assistance in exchange for significant oil exploration rights in oil-rich but poor African and Latin American nations. Erica Downs of The Brookings Institution notes that, "in the first half of 2009 alone, Chinese banks extended more than $45 billion in loans to countries including Brazil, Kazakhstan, Russia, and Venezuela, all major energy producers battered by the fall in oil prices."

Chinese national oil companies are forced to seek oil from impoverished, dangerous nations because the United States and other OECD [Organisation for Economic Co-operation and Development] nations have long-term contracts for oil from "friendlier" nations. . . .

China isn't the only country eyeing oil abroad. Indian oil companies are aggressively pursuing overseas energy deals. The country just reached an oil exploration deal with Angola and is seeking deals with other unstable developing nations such as Nigeria and Sudan. Saudi Arabia, the world's largest crude oil supplier, increased its exports to India sevenfold between 2000 and 2008 and announced in February 2010 that it would nearly double its crude exports to India this year [2010], up to 770,000 barrels per day from last year [2009].

China, India, and other growing economies have responded to increased global demand by securing more energy sources in a variety of different ways. Additionally, China has heavily invested in oil demand reduction strategies for vehicles such as fuel economy standards that are more efficient than those in the United States, aggressive

> **FAST FACT**
>
> *National Geographic* reports that Americans drink about 29 billion bottles of water every year, which requires the use of 17 million barrels of crude oil. That is equivalent to the fuel used by 1 million vehicles in twelve months.

electric vehicle plans and plug-in hybrid deployment, and increased efficiency and technology programs. Japan and India have had to aggressively pursue stricter fuel efficiency standards, too.

## The Price of Oil Is Breaking the Bank

Worldwide oil demand growth will cause economic harm to Americans if left unaddressed. Growing foreign demand combined with U.S. demand will produce rising oil prices—something we're already beginning to see with oil prices recently hitting an 18-month high of $87 per barrel in April 2010. . . .

Higher oil prices will mean higher prices at the gas pump. The EIA [U.S. Energy Information Administration] forecasts that average gasoline prices will exceed $3.00 per gallon by this spring [2010]. Drivers will pay 17 percent more for gas compared to summer 2009—$174 million per day, or an average of $602 per household annually. Energy price volatility like this hurts consumer and business investments, causing families to delay buying a car and spend less on buying or upgrading their homes. Businesses also cut investments, while profits surge in the oil and gas industry.

## Oil Exploration Causes Devastation and Tragedy

The United States consumes more than 7 billion barrels of oil annually, but expanding domestic oil production will not solve our supply problem, make us more secure, or ease our wallets. President Barack Obama made it clear that drilling is not the solution to America's energy challenges, explaining, "We have less than 2 percent of the world's oil reserves; we consume more than 20 percent of the world's oil. . . . Drilling alone can't come close to meeting our long-term energy needs."

The United States does not have enough accessible nationwide reserves to meet our energy demand, and there is also great uncertainty over how much recoverable oil does exist. Supplies of extractable oil are dwindling. The amount of oil in proven U.S. reserves has steadily decreased since the 1970s, from 31.8 billion barrels to 21 billion barrels in 2007.

Drilling for oil in the Arctic National Wildlife Refuge in Alaska and areas formerly off limits in the Outer Continental Shelf [OCS] will not close the supply gap. The amount of recoverable oil in the Arctic

# More Countries Need More Oil

Rapidly developing countries like China and India consume more oil as they grow. Experts worry this additional demand will place extra strain on already strapped oil reserves, making oil run out even faster than previously thought.

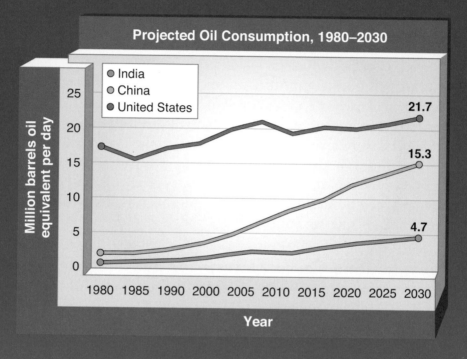

**Projected Oil Consumption, 1980–2030**

- India
- China
- United States

21.7

15.3

4.7

Million barrels oil equivalent per day

1980 1985 1990 2000 2005 2010 2015 2020 2025 2030

Year

Taken from: Susan Lyon, Rebecca Lefton, and Daniel J. Weiss. "Quenching Our Thirst for Oil." Center for American Progress, April 23, 2010. Based on data from the Energy Information Administration.

coastal plain is estimated to be between 5.7 billion and 16 billion barrels. This could supply as little as a year's worth of oil. And it will take 10 years to produce any oil from this supply. The OCS has only slightly more recoverable oil.

The areas that became open for offshore oil production in 2008 have only a small portion of U.S. reserves. EIA determined that "the OCS areas that were until recently under moratoria in the Atlantic, Pacific, and Eastern/Central Gulf of Mexico are estimated to hold roughly 20 percent (18 billion barrels) of the total OCS technically recoverable oil." As with the Arctic, EIA predicts that "conversion of the newly available OCS resources to production will require considerable time, in addition to financial investment." And the horrible tragedy at the Gulf Coast oil rig[1] reminds us of the potential human cost of offshore oil production. . . .

The United States needs comprehensive clean energy and climate policies to decrease our dependence on this expensive and unstable commodity. . . . If we fail to reduce our oil consumption, energy costs will hurt national security and Americans' pocketbooks. We can take immediate steps to create oil savings that we know work. We must also take the lead in developing and producing oil savings with vehicles of the future, and we can profit by marketing these products to the world.

## EVALUATING THE AUTHOR'S ARGUMENTS:

Susan Lyon, Rebecca Lefton, and Daniel J. Weiss view oil as a deeply problematic resource that is responsible for causing war, conflict, economic hardship, and environmental damage. Alex Epstein, author of the following viewpoint, views oil as a deeply useful resource, responsible for humanity's most important developments, inventions, and achievements. After reading both viewpoints, with which view do you ultimately agree? Why?

---

1. In which eleven workers died in an explosion on the *Deepwater Horizon* in April 2010. Nearly 4.9 million barrels of oil were spilled into the Gulf of Mexico.

# Let's Celebrate Oil's 150th Birthday and the Value It Adds to Our Lives

## Alex Epstein

*"Nearly every item in your life would either not exist or be far more expensive without oil."*

Alex Epstein is the founder of the Center for Industrial Progress, which champions oil as the world's premier energy source. In the following viewpoint he argues that oil is not a problematic resource—on the contrary, it is responsible for all of humanity's most important developments, inventions, and achievements. Oil is used in everything from medicine to technology, food safety, and transportation. Epstein says products and inventions derived from oil have collectively made billions of people safer, healthier, more comfortable, richer, and happier. He thinks people should feel thankful for oil, but instead they resent it and demonize it. Epstein says oil should be celebrated and credited with uplifting the human experience, rather than being looked down upon as a problem.

**AS YOU READ, CONSIDER THE FOLLOWING QUESTIONS:**

1. How much did a gallon of whale oil cost in 1860? How does this compare to kerosene (an oil-based product) in 1880?
2. What role did oil play in World Wars I and II, according to Epstein?
3. List at least three life-improving inventions the author attributes to oil.

Thursday marked the 150th anniversary of a seminal event in history: the birth of the oil industry. On that day in 1859, Edwin Drake struck black gold with the first commercial oil well—creating an industry that would provide the lifeblood for modern civilization.

And yet no one seems to care.

In previous generations, the birth of the oil industry was celebrated, and deservedly so. Oil has sustained and enhanced billions of lives for more than 150 years by providing superior, affordable, ultraconvenient energy—and is as vital today as ever.

*Early oil production began in the 1860s and mostly produced kerosene for lighting.*

The oil industry began its ascent by dominating the fast-growing illumination energy market of the 1860s. Producers of oil-based kerosene won out due to superior quality and price. Where whale oil was lighting homes for $3 a gallon in 1860, kerosene was lighting homes for 9 cents a gallon by 1880—giving millions of Americans the gift of illumination at night.

In the early 20th century, as the electric light bulb outcompeted kerosene, oil producers focused on producing automotive fuel—and beat out steam, ethanol and—the front-runner at the time—electric batteries, through a combination of affordability, safety and convenience.

The availability of cheap, personalized transport is something oil makes possible, and something we should never take for granted.

As a gasoline marketer told a group of gas station attendants in 1928: "My friends, it is the juice of the fountain of eternal youth that you are selling. It is health. It is comfort. It is success. . . . You must put yourself in the place of the man and woman in whose lives your gasoline has worked miracles."

Oil also worked miracles for America's military in World Wars I and II. Vehicles powered by ample quantities of the most portable, highest-energy-density fuel gave them the enormous advantage of superior speed and mobility.

Many historians have argued that Allied nations' superior ability to produce oil was a decisive factor in both wars. In war, as in economics, having the cheapest, most convenient energy is a matter of life and death.

Today, oil brings even more value to our lives.

One underappreciated form is petroleum-based products. We live in a world where chemists are able to employ oil to suit any conceivable purpose, from making shatterproof glasses to ultra-durable synthetic rubber tires to medical implants to bacteria-resistant refrigerators to HDTVs to iPhones. Look in your home and you can find 100 things made of oil in no time.

One barrel of crude oil (which is 42 gallons), is refined into many useful products.

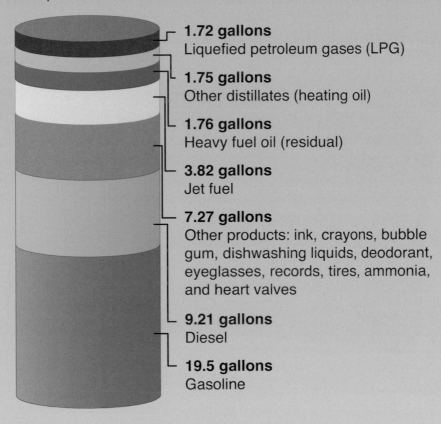

**1.72 gallons**
Liquefied petroleum gases (LPG)

**1.75 gallons**
Other distillates (heating oil)

**1.76 gallons**
Heavy fuel oil (residual)

**3.82 gallons**
Jet fuel

**7.27 gallons**
Other products: ink, crayons, bubble gum, dishwashing liquids, deodorant, eyeglasses, records, tires, ammonia, and heart valves

**9.21 gallons**
Diesel

**19.5 gallons**
Gasoline

Taken from: U.S. Energy Information Administration; Lehigh University.

Nearly every item in your life would either not exist or be far more expensive without oil; there is simply no comparable source of practical, portable energy.

Yet today people increasingly label oil a pollutant that damages rather than enhances our lives and, even worse, an addiction—likening our consumption of oil to a junkie's self-destructive heroin habit. This is profoundly ignorant, not to mention unfair to the petroleum industry that tirelessly innovates, year after year, to find more oil and extract it more efficiently.

Does this mean that no one should look for alternatives to oil? Of course entrepreneurs should—if they believe that they can truly match or exceed oil's value in the market. For example, if a liberated nuclear industry can provide ultracheap electric power that makes petroleum the whale oil of the 21st century, that will be something to celebrate.

Today, though, we should be celebrating petroleum—"the juice of the fountain of eternal youth"—and the industry, past and present, that uses it to work miracles in our lives.

## EVALUATING THE AUTHOR'S ARGUMENTS:

Alex Epstein offers a unique perspective on oil, saying that humans should feel thankful for it and credit it with improving nearly every aspect of their lives. He even suggests that people be more appreciative of the oil industry. What is your opinion of this perspective? Is it a fair assessment of oil's role in human development? Explain your reasoning.

# Oil Use Undermines National Security

### Truman National Security Project

> "Depending on oil to run our nation makes America vulnerable, while paying enormous sums to those who could do us harm."

The Truman National Security Project is a leadership institute that trains Americans to lead on national security issues. In the following viewpoint analysts at the project argue that being dependent on oil undermines US national security in several critical ways. First, it leaves the United States at the mercy of the countries from which it buys oil, preventing it from making neutral, unbiased policy decisions. In addition, many of the countries that sell oil to the United States are dangerous, unstable, or unfriendly. By purchasing their oil, the United States counterproductively funds and strengthens its enemies. Access to oil has also embroiled the United States in several long and costly wars, which puts US national security at risk. Finally, the authors say that oil use contributes to climate change, which in turn causes war, political instability, food and resource scarcity, and other destabilizing events. For all of these reasons, they believe that oil use undermines national security and should be abandoned in the interests of a safe, strong America.

1. According to the authors, what percentage of oil imports comes from nations that pose the greatest security risk to the United States?
2. How much money would a five-dollar increase in the global price of oil send to the nation of Iran, according to the authors?
3. Name three specific examples of how climate change contributes to war, instability, or resource scarcity, as described by the authors.

Americans depend on their cars for over 90% of all travel. Those cars are fueled almost entirely (94%) by oil. Depending on oil to run our nation makes America vulnerable, while paying enormous sums to those who could do us harm. It is time for America to take control of its energy future, cut dependence on oil, and defund terrorist threats. Increasing fuel economy to 60 miles per gallon by 2025 is a major step to bolster U.S. security.

## Oil Dependency Threatens National Security

The U.S. sends nearly $1 billion a day overseas to import oil. This staggering figure has dangerous national security implications. Scaling back the magnitude of our oil addiction will allow America to reduce dependency on oil supplies from countries that don't share our values. By tackling our oil addiction, we reduce economic waste, environmental damage, political complications, and military involvement.

America depends heavily on troubled nations who are (or have recently been) on the U.S. State Department travel advisory due to long-term, protracted turmoil. The nations that pose the greatest security risk to the U.S. account for 43% of U.S. oil imports. Reducing U.S. dependence on the most dangerous or unstable nations for nearly one-half of U.S. oil supplies is prudent and in our long-term strategic interests.

In 1973, OPEC [Organization of the Petroleum Exporting Countries] nations caused our economy to grind to a halt with an oil embargo. At the time, the U.S. only imported 35% of its oil. Today U.S. oil imports have more than doubled. Barring the current economic downturn, U.S. oil imports have increased unabated since the mid-1980s, despite oil crises, political skirmishes, and wars in the Middle East. America's long-term goal should be to reduce its oil demands, closing the gap and ultimately eliminate the need to import oil.

## Buying Oil from Unfriendly Nations

The United States imports nearly half of its crude oil from nations on the State Department's travel warning list. Some worry that sending so much money to unfriendly or uncooperative nations undermines national security.

| US Imported Crude Oil from Nations on State Department's Travel Warning List | |
|---|---|
| Country | Crude Oil Imports (barrels per day) |
| Mauritania | 4,000 |
| Syria | 9,000 |
| Chad | 24,000 |
| Democratic Republic of Congo | 82,000 |
| Azerbaijan | 90,000 |
| Colombia | 407,000 |
| Algeria | 550,000 |
| Iraq | 630,000 |
| Nigeria | 1,109,000 |
| Mexico | 1,208,000 |
| Saudi Arabia | 1,353,000 |
| **Subtotal Security–Risk Nations** | **5,466,000** |
| **Total US Oil Imports** | **12,590,000** |

Taken from: Truman National Security Project. "Tackling Oil Addiction," October 2010.

## Better Standards Could Bolster Security

New Corporate Average Fuel Economy (CAFE) standards of 60 mpg by 2025 could help reduce America's oil addiction. By 2030, as 60-mpg cars spread through the market, the U.S. could cut one in every four barrels of oil imports. The oil savings resulting from a 60-mpg CAFE standard are equivalent to an estimated 58 percent of current U.S. crude oil imports from OPEC. This could eliminate about one in every 2 barrels of the U.S.' OPEC imports, at current supply levels. These savings are even more remarkable considering just U.S. imports from Persian Gulf nations. A 60-mpg fuel economy standard could free the U.S. entirely from Persian Gulf and Venezuelan crude oil imports, reducing dependency on potential enemies and defunding individuals and nations that support extremist groups.

These savings will keep growing as new, fuel-efficient cars enter the market. Given that OPEC nations control the vast majority of the world's oil supplies the only viable way to reduce U.S. dependence on these nations is to reduce American demand for petroleum.

Adopting a 60-mpg standard is projected to save over $140 billion a year spent on foreign oil by 2030. Oil is also creating a foreign trade deficit that is greater than the current (year-to-date) U.S. deficit with China as of July 2010. In addition to keeping billions of dollars at home, the savings from a 60-mpg fuel economy standard could eliminate the deficit in our current oil trade balance. The estimated 50 billion gallons saved annually by 2030 are projected to put $180 billion back into Americans' pockets, and possibly more if gasoline prices rise higher than projected in the future.

## All Oil Sources Have Security Risks

Oil has proved to be political oxygen for dictatorships and hostile nations. In his first term, as world gas prices rose, Iranian President Mahmoud Ahmadinejad benefited from a windfall of $250 billion in oil sales. Oil wealth funded about 60% of the Iranian national budget in 2008. Likewise, in Venezuela, oil pays for what Hugo Chavez calls, "21st century socialism" and finances anti-American alliances between Venezuela, Bolivia, Nicaragua, and El Salvador.

The price of oil is set globally. That means that even when we buy oil from friendly countries, like Canada, we drive up demand, inflating prices that enrich those hostile to our interests. The U.S.' immense appetite for oil bolsters dictators despite trade sanctions. And when oil prices fall, as they have since their high in 2008, this can destabilize nations that depend on oil to fund the majority of their national budgets. Many of these nations are already struggling with internal political tensions and social disruption, increasing the chances that oil-driven economic downturns could lead to regime failure or extremist empowerment. There are significant security risks whether the price of oil is high or low.

## Sending Money to Our Enemies

Every $5 increase in the global price of oil represents:

- An additional $7.9 billion for Iran and President Ahmadinejad
- An additional $4.7 billion for Venezuela and President Chavez
- An additional $18 billion for Russia and President Medvedev

Even if America drilled every untapped well at home, we simply do not have enough oil to offset OPEC's pricing power or to fuel ever increasing domestic demand. America only has 1.5% of the world's oil reserves, estimated at 21 billion barrels. Reserve estimates are based on reasonable recovery under existing economic and operating conditions. Even if tomorrow's technological capabilities and economic factors facilitate tapping more oil, Alaskan and deepwater oil in the Gulf are not expected to relieve U.S. dependence on oil imports. By staying addicted to oil, regardless of where we purchase it, we give OPEC countries the power to cripple our economy and bring America to its knees.

Even Canada cannot save us in our quest to procure safe oil. While more stable and friendly than any other oil trade partner, relying on Canada for vast sums of oil may actually do more harm than good. Today, Canada is the U.S.' largest oil trade partner at 2.7 million barrels of oil per day in June

> ## FAST FACT
>
> According to the Sierra Club, 68 percent of the petroleum imported by the United States comes from "very high risk" or "high risk" countries—that is, countries that are politically unstable, violent, or otherwise risky to rely on or do business with.

*Truman National Security Project fellow Drew Sloan testifies before the US Congress about the country's energy future, saying the United States is too dependent on foreign oil.*

2010. America imports more oil from its North American neighbor than any other country, including Saudi Arabia, the nation with the world's largest oil reserves. This may reduce dependence on OPEC, but relying on high-carbon Canadian tar sands as a fossil fuels source, while feeding our domestic oil addiction, increases the risks associated with climate disruption.

## Climate Security Is National Security

Military experts caution that climate change is a threat multiplier, accelerating conflict through climatic events such as droughts and floods, and the resulting famines and crop failures. These warnings have gone unheeded. Cutting carbon from America's gas-guzzling vehicle fleet has proven difficult. From 1990 to 2008, car and light truck greenhouse gas (GHG) emissions increased 20 percent. Business-as-usual oil consumption is extremely problematic for the climate. A 60-mpg fuel economy standard is estimated to cut 535 million metric tons of $CO_2$-equivalent GHG emissions annually in 2030.

Climate change is likely to create new geopolitical dilemmas as waterways, resources, and precipitation levels shift. Military operations would be affected as bases near waterways are inundated. Empirical evidence suggests that climate change can cause domestic and international conflict. Long-term fluctuations of global wars and death rates are correlated with shifts in temperatures. According to the UNEP [United Nations Environment Programme], military conflict in Darfur has been exacerbated by climate change, with extreme droughts and creeping desertification resulting in up to 500,000 deaths. Scientists have determined that long-term fluctuations of war frequently followed cycles of temperature change.

Expanding oil supplies at home will make us less secure due to greater climate effects. The ultra-deep oil trapped in the Gulf of Mexico, over 5 miles below the surface, requires significantly more energy to produce under extreme conditions. Likewise, the oil trapped in shale in the Rocky Mountains is enormously energy intensive to produce. The U.S. is no more secure drilling at home, as domestic oil supplies drive up carbon emissions. A 60-mpg fuel economy standard could cut passenger vehicle greenhouse gas emissions by over 50 percent.

## Climate Change Contributes to War and Insecurity

Climate change, and its resultant weather effect, is directly connected to national security. Military experts underscore the potential for climate-induced food and water shortages contributing to political instability, which could be exploited by extremists. Extreme weather conditions that lead to mass migrations are expected to be "threat multipliers."

A panel of eleven former generals and admirals stated that climate change, national security, and energy dependence are a related set of global challenges. In 2010, an unprecedented 33 retired Generals and Admirals announced their support for comprehensive climate legislation. Many former military leaders have lobbied Congress to regulate GHG emissions and advance clean domestic energy alternatives (including reducing fuel consumption through significantly improved vehicle fuel economy) to help us confront the serious challenge of global climate change.

## The Road to Security

A 60-mpg fuel economy standard beginning in 2025 will cut our addiction to fossil fuels, boost clean energy technology, and move our nation dramatically toward greater energy independence. This policy is vital to our national security, to the safety of our men and women in uniform, and to the fight against terrorism.

The need is immediate. Increasing fuel economy standards to 60 mpg must be our overarching goal. Our national security depends on the swift, serious, and thoughtful response to the inter-linked challenges of energy security and climate change.

> **EVALUATING THE AUTHOR'S ARGUMENTS:**
>
> Analysts at the Truman National Security Project argue that when the United States imports oil, it sends money to unfriendly countries and may even fund terrorism. How does Robert Bryce, author of the following viewpoint, directly respond to this claim? After reading both viewpoints, state with which author you agree, and why. What piece of evidence swayed you? It could be the identity of an author, a fact or opinion expressed in one of the viewpoints, or another piece of evidence.

# Oil Use Does Not Undermine National Security

**Viewpoint**

**4**

*"The conflation of oil prices and terrorism makes no sense for one simple reason: terrorism is a cheap endeavor."*

**Robert Bryce**

Oil use does not fund terrorism or leave the United States at the mercy of unfriendly governments, argues Robert Bryce in the following viewpoint. Bryce is annoyed that for decades, US politicians, commentators, and analysts have called America's oil use a national security threat. He says money spent on oil does not fund terrorist attacks—such attacks are very cheap to orchestrate, he points out, and terrorists do not need oil dollars to carry out their crimes. Furthermore, Bryce says terrorists are isolated individuals who are not connected to the oil industry or to petrostate, or oil-exporting, governments. In addition, Bryce argues that the fact that America imports some of its oil does not affect its security, because of the global nature of the oil market. Oil sellers need customers, and there are so many oil sellers that nations can choose where they buy oil. So the United States could not be held at the mercy of any one particular government. Finally, Bryce says the United States is itself a major oil exporter, so claims that it is entirely dependent on foreign sources of oil are false. He urges Americans to lay to rest the falsehood that using oil is in any way connected to national security. Bryce writes frequently about energy, politics, and other issues. His articles have been published in the *New York Times*, the *Wall Street Journal*, the *Washington Post*, and other major news outlets.

**AS YOU READ, CONSIDER THE FOLLOWING QUESTIONS:**
1. How much did it cost terrorists to execute the September 11 terrorist attacks? How does this factor into Bryce's argument?
2. What year does Bryce say America began importing significant amounts of crude oil? What bearing does this have on his argument?
3. Who is Keith Crane? How does he factor into the author's argument?

Politicians and pundits continually use the price shocks of the 1970s[1] to justify their claims that the US could suddenly be cut off from global oil supplies. And that fear has been used to justify a myriad of wasteful government programs, among them, the corn ethanol scam, one of the most misguided and costly subsidies in modern American history. And in the wake of the September 11 attacks[2] the calls for more alternative fuels and increased efforts to reduce the use of oil, have surged. Those calls are coming from the both the Left and the Right, with both claiming that using less oil will mean less terrorism.

## Oil Use Does Not Invite Terrorism

The claimed rationale for using less oil is simple: if the US consumes less, then the price of oil will fall, petrostates [countries that export oil] who have ties to terrorism will have less money and therefore terrorism

---

1. The author is referring to oil embargoes, in which oil was used as a political weapon against the United States.
2. Nearly three thousand Americans were killed in the September 11, 2001, attacks against the United States that were carried out by terrorists who were largely from Saudi Arabia, a major oil exporter.

will decline. This thesis has already been tested. And it has been proven false. Between about 1986 and 2000, oil prices generally stayed below $20 per barrel. By the end of 1998, prices had fallen as low as $11 per barrel. On September 11, 2001, the day of the al-Qaeda attacks on the U.S., the price of oil was $27.65. Where is the link between high oil prices and terrorism?

We had terrorism when oil was selling for less than $30 per barrel. And we will have it if oil ever sells for more than $300. The conflation of oil prices and terrorism makes no sense for one simple reason: terrorism is a cheap endeavor. The 9-11 attacks cost about $500,000. Terrorist organizations don't need the backing of the petrostates in order to launch their attacks. Furthermore, even if the US quits buying oil, it won't mean an end to the flow of money to the petrostates. According to the Energy Information Administration, out of the 204 countries and territories that they track, 173 are net oil importers. If the U.S. quits buying oil, there are 172 other countries on the planet who will enjoy cheaper oil. And they will buy it from the lowest cost oil producer. . . .

## The United States Is Not Dependent on Oil Imports

Most energy analysts focus on the level of US oil imports. Few bother to look at the amount of oil leaving US ports. Over the past few years the US has become one of the world's biggest exporters of refined products. In 1998, the US was exporting about 945,000 barrels of oil and refined oil products per day. By 2008, the US was exporting nearly twice that amount, some 1.8 million barrels per day. And through the first six months of 2009, those exports have continued, with daily exports averaging 1.9 million barrels per day. At that level, US oil exports are on par with countries like Angola and Venezuela.

Of course, the vast majority of those exports are refined products, not crude. But why has the US become a major player in the international oil market for refined products? The answer: US refineries are among the best in the world. And those refineries can produce the types of fuels the global market demands. One of the largest elements of US oil exports involves distillate fuel oil, much of which is going to customers in Europe and South America. Buyers in those regions are eager to purchase low-sulfur diesel fuel. Europe has a shortage of diesel refining capacity and given that US refiners can supply the needed product, European buyers are relying on the US to make up for their shortfall.

## The World Oil Market Is Intertwined

While America's role as an oil exporter is partly a function of its position as the world's biggest oil importer, it's also true that the US refining sector is bolstering its role as a global player in manufactured goods. That can be seen by looking at crude oil import levels. In 1998, US crude oil and petroleum product imports averaged 10.7 million barrels per day. By 2008, that number had increased to 12.9 million barrels per day. Thus, while total US imports increased by 2.2 million barrels per day over that time period, the amount of US exports of refined products doubled to 1.8 million barrels per day.

The fundamental point here is obvious: the US cannot secede from the global oil market. It has always been a major player in global oil trade and it will continue being a major player for decades to come.

## Oil Importing Is an Old Practice

In recent years, T. Boone Pickens [a businessperson who is critical of the oil industry], [columnist] Thomas Friedman of the *New York Times*, and various other high-profile individuals have sounded the alarm

**FAST FACT**

According to the US Energy Information Administration, the top supplier of US crude oil is Canada, which sends 2,658,000 barrels of oil per day to the United States, as of March 1, 2013.

about America's oil imports. Alas, they are a little late to the game. The US has been a net crude oil importer since 1913. In fact, between 1913 and 2008, the U.S. was a net crude exporter in just nine of those years. In 1913—just five years after Henry Ford began selling his Model T—America was importing 36,000 barrels of crude oil per day. Nine decades later, in 2005, with [President] George W. Bush in the White House, the U.S. was importing almost 300 times as much oil as it did when Woodrow Wilson was living at 1600 Pennsylvania Avenue [the address of the White House].

*Traders work in the crude oil options pit at the New York Mercantile Exchange. Between 1986 and 2000, oil prices stayed below twenty dollars a barrel despite various terrorist attacks around the world, which supports the theory that terrorism does not significantly affect the oil market.*

But those numbers must be put in perspective. Over the past century or so, America's energy consumption has grown in direct relation to its economic growth: In 1913, America's gross domestic product [GDP] was about $39 billion. By 2005, U.S. GDP was more than $12.4 trillion, or about 300 times as much as the 1913 figure. Thus, in a remarkable parallel, that 300-fold increase in oil imports has been accompanied by a 300-fold increase in America's economic output.

Despite the long history of US imports, US politicians continue to stoke fears about oil imports and the possibility of another oil embargo. For instance, in 2006, [former president] Bill Clinton gave a speech in California during which he said "Think of the instability and the impotence you feel knowing that every day we have to have a lifeline from places half a world away that could cut us off in a minute."

More than half of all US oil imports came from Western nations; less than a quarter comes from countries in the Middle East.

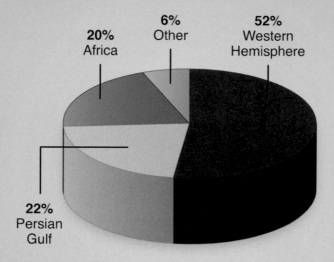

Taken from: US Energy Information Administration. *Petroleum Supply Monthly*, February 2012.

## Imported Oil Poses No Security Threat

Of course, any time Bill Clinton uses the word "impotence" is worth noting. But a May 2009 report by the Rand Corporation [a think tank] thoroughly debunks this type of rhetoric. "The fact that the United States imports nearly three-fifths of its oil does not pose a national security threat," said Keith Crane, the study's lead author and senior economist at Rand. "There is an integrated world oil market, and embargoes do not work."

Few people would consider the Rand Corporation as soft on defense. The think tank has been a powerful player in the US defense establishment for more than six decades. (Daniel Ellsberg, the author of the Pentagon Papers [a controversial U.S. Department of Defense report], worked at Rand.) And yet Rand concludes that "reliance on imported oil is not by itself a major national security threat." Just as important, the Rand study also debunks the conflation of oil prices and terrorism. Crane and his co-authors conclude that "Terrorist attacks cost so little to perpetrate that attempting to curtail terrorist financing through measures affecting the oil market will not be effective.". . . .

## The United States Cannot Be Held Hostage, Because Oil Producers Need Customers

Of course, we live in a global economy, particularly when it comes to energy. The petrostates of the Persian Gulf and elsewhere must sell their oil. They can't drink it or use it to water their geraniums. The same holds true for the countries that produce lithium, neodymium, and rare elements. And given the ongoing globalization of the world economy, it stands to reason that the marketplace will help assure that buyers and sellers will reach an agreed-upon price for whatever goods or services are on offer. That said, the difference between the hyper-global oil sector and the near-monopoly that China has on the rare earths market business is akin to the difference between aluminum and dysprosium.

In summary, the reality of the energy sector is this: energy security—whatever the favored definition for that term—means interdependence. And that interdependence goes far beyond energy commodities like diesel fuel, gasoline, natural gas, and neodymium. The US is a vital player in the global marketplace for a myriad of commodities, ranging from iPods and tennis rackets to fresh flowers and bottled water. The sooner the US discards the hypertrophied rhetoric about energy security and energy independence and accepts the reality of our interdependence, the more secure and prosperous it will be.

**EVALUATING THE AUTHOR'S ARGUMENTS:**

Robert Bryce quotes from several sources to support the points he makes in his viewpoint. Make a list of everyone he quotes, including their credentials and the nature of their comments. Then, analyze the sources—are they credible? Are they well qualified to speak on this subject? What specific points do they support?

# The Americas, Not the Middle East, Will Be the World Capital of Energy

**Amy Myers Jaffe**

> *"America may be back in the energy leadership saddle again."*

In the following viewpoint Amy Myers Jaffe argues that after decades of relying on foreign countries, the United States is on the brink of producing enough of its own oil to be considered energy independent. She discusses how advances in technology, such as horizontal drilling (which helps extract oil from deep in the ocean) and shale gas production (which squeezes oil from a kind of rock called shale), have helped the United States—and other North and South American countries—extract millions of barrels of oil from unconventional oil reserves estimated at trillions of barrels. Jaffe says these developments coincide with a decline in production in traditional Middle Eastern petrostates like Iran and Libya, due in part to supply and in part to political troubles.

Jaffe predicts the next several decades will witness a critical transition of power, as North America takes the reins on the world's energy industry. The author encourages Americans to seize the opportunity and become the capital of the global energy industry. Jaffe is the former Wallace S. Wilson Fellow in Energy Studies at the James A. Baker III Institute for Public Policy at Rice University in Houston, Texas.

**AS YOU READ, CONSIDER THE FOLLOWING QUESTIONS:**
1. How many barrels of unconventional oil does the author say exist in US territory?
2. What percentage of US natural gas is currently supplied by shale gas that is domestically produced? What percentage does the author say will be supplied by domestic resources by 2040?
3. How much shale oil do analysts predict will be found under the Great Plains and Texas?

For half a century, the global energy supply's center of gravity has been the Middle East. This fact has had self-evidently enormous implications for the world we live in—and it's about to change.

By the 2020s, the capital of energy will likely have shifted back to the Western Hemisphere, where it was prior to the ascendancy of Middle Eastern megasuppliers such as Saudi Arabia and Kuwait in the 1960s. The reasons for this shift are partly technological and partly political. Geologists have long known that the Americas are home to plentiful hydrocarbons trapped in hard-to-reach offshore deposits, on-land shale rock, oil sands, and heavy oil formations. The U.S. endowment of unconventional oil is more than 2 trillion barrels, with another 2.4 trillion in Canada and 2 trillion-plus in South America—compared with conventional Middle Eastern and North African oil resources of 1.2 trillion. The problem was always how to unlock them economically.

But since the early 2000s, the energy industry has largely solved that problem. With the help of horizontal drilling and other innovations, shale gas production in the United States has skyrocketed from virtually nothing to 15 to 20 percent of the U.S. natural gas supply in less than a decade. By 2040, it could account for more than half of it. This tremendous change in volume has turned the conversation in the U.S. natural gas industry on its head; where Americans once fretted about meeting the country's natural gas needs, they now worry about finding potential buyers for the country's surplus.

Meanwhile, onshore oil production in the United States, condemned to predictions of inexorable decline by analysts for two decades, is about to stage an unexpected comeback. Oil production from shale rock, a technically complex process of squeezing hydrocarbons from sedimentary deposits, is just beginning. But analysts are predicting production of as much as 1.5 million barrels a day in the next few years from resources beneath the Great Plains and Texas alone—the equivalent of 8 percent of current U.S. oil consumption. The development raises the question of what else the U.S. energy industry might accomplish if prices remain high and technology continues to advance. Rising recovery rates from old wells, for example, could also stem previous declines. On top of all this, analysts expect an additional 1 to 2 million barrels a day from the Gulf of Mexico now that drilling is resuming. Peak oil? Not anytime soon.

The picture elsewhere in the Americas is similarly promising. Brazil is believed to have the capacity to pump 2 million barrels a day from "pre-salt" deepwater resources, deposits of crude found more than a mile below the surface of the Atlantic Ocean that until the last couple of years were technologically inaccessible. Similar gains are to be had in Canadian oil sands, where petroleum is extracted from tarry sediment in open pits. And production of perhaps 3 million to 7 million barrels a day more is possible if U.S. *in situ* heavy oil, or kerogen, can be produced commercially, a process that involves heating rock to allow the oil contained within it to be pumped out in a liquid form. There is no question that such developments face environmental hurdles. But industry is starting to see that it must find ways to get over them, investing in nontoxic drilling fluids, less-invasive hydraulic-fracturing

## FAST FACT

*U.S. News & World Report* claims that by 2022, the United States will produce so much of its own fossil fuels that it will be able to cut petroleum imports from 10 million barrels per day down to 3 million barrels per day.

*Advanced drilling technology has enabled more oil to be extracted from deep sources than was possible with previous drilling rigs.*

techniques, and new water-recycling processes, among other technologies, in hopes of shrinking the environmental impact of drilling. And like the U.S. oil industry, oil-thirsty China has also recognized the energy potential of the Americas, investing billions in Canada, the United States, and Latin America.

The revolution-swept Middle East and North Africa, meanwhile, will soon be facing up to an inconvenient truth about their own fossil-fuel legacy: Changes of government in the region have historically led to long and steep declines in oil production. Libya's oil output has never recovered to the 3.5 million barrels a day it was producing when Col. Muammar al-Qaddafi overthrew King Idris in 1969; instead it has been stuck at under 2 million barrels a day for three decades and is now close to zero. Iran produced more than 6 million barrels a day in the times of the shah but saw oil production fall precipitously below 2 million barrels a day in the aftermath of the 1979 Islamic Revolution.

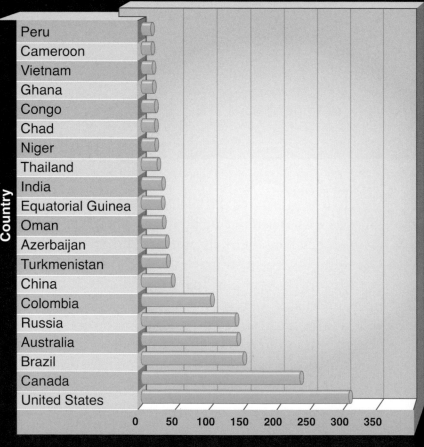

**Thousand Barrels per Day**

It failed to recover significantly during the 1980s and has only crept back to 4 million in recent years. Iraq's production has also suffered during its many years of turmoil and now sits at 2.7 million barrels a day, lower than the 3.5 million it produced before Saddam Hussein came to power.

The Arab Spring stands to complicate matters even further: A 1979-style disruption in Middle Eastern oil exports is hardly out of the question, nor are work stoppages or strikes by oil workers caught up in the region's political Zeitgeist. All in all, upwards of 21 million barrels a day of Arab oil production are at stake—about a quarter of global demand. The boom in the Americas, meanwhile, should be food for thought for the Middle East's remaining autocrats: It means they may not be able to count on ever-rising oil prices to calm restive populations.

This hydrocarbon-driven reordering of geopolitics is already taking place. The petropower of Iran, Russia, and Venezuela has faltered on the back of plentiful American natural gas supply: A surplus of resources in the Americas is sending other foreign suppliers scrambling to line up buyers in Europe and Asia, making it more difficult for such exporters to assert themselves via heavy-handed energy "diplomacy." The U.S. energy industry may also be able to provide the technical assistance necessary for Europe and China to tap unconventional resources of their own, scuttling their need to kowtow to Moscow or the Persian Gulf. So watch this space: America may be back in the energy leadership saddle again.

### EVALUATING THE AUTHOR'S ARGUMENTS:

In this viewpoint Amy Myers Jaffe uses facts, statistics, examples, and reasoning to make her argument that the United States is about to become energy independent. She does not, however, use any quotations to support her points. If you were to rewrite this article and insert quotations, what authorities might you quote from? Where would you place quotations, and why?

# The United States Should Not Desire Energy Independence

**Dave Shellenberger**

*"The notion that energy independence is desirable is just another trade myth."*

The United States should not want to become energy independent, argues Dave Shellenberger in the following viewpoint. He explains that politicians, analysts, and others have long said energy independence can solve America's political, economic, environmental, and national security problems. But Shellenberger argues these claims are false: Buying oil from foreign sources does not make the United States more vulnerable to terrorism, nor does it make it negatively reliant on other countries. In addition, he says domestic sources of energy are not as powerful as oil, and promoting them simply for the sake of claiming energy independence is wasteful. Finally, Shellenberger says that being energy independent would hurt the United States economically, because it would prevent the country from trading on the global market, which has vast financial benefits. For all of these reasons, he says the United States should rethink why it wants to become energy independent and realize that doing so would ultimately hurt the country. Shellenberger is a lawyer and analyst who writes articles on energy, economics, and other political subjects.

**AS YOU READ, CONSIDER THE FOLLOWING QUESTIONS:**
1. What percentage of oil in the world market does Shellenberger say comes from nations that have been accused of funding terrorism?
2. What main problem does Shellenberger have with ethanol and biofuels?
3. What does Shellenberger say the government would do if it truly believed that switching to biofuels would benefit the environment? What bearing does this have on his argument?

P eople seem to be peculiarly susceptible to economic myths, including those related to trade. The notion that energy independence is desirable is just another trade myth. The proponents favor expanded government, protection of domestic producers, and subsidies to alternative energy interests.

The need for energy independence is usually rationalized by three justifications: avoiding "transferring wealth" to hostile nations, providing security to prevent the cut-off of supplies, and obtaining the environmental benefits of alternative energy. Each basis is wrong.

## Participating in Trade Is Healthy
One reason the idea of energy independence is wrong on its face is that it implicitly rejects free trade. Free trade always benefits both parties to the trade, and this is true for energy, as it is for bananas, cotton, wheat, steel, and any other commodity, product, or service. Seeking independence in anything, whether it is India regarding food, or the U.S. regarding energy, is an indulgence of the mercantilist myth that there is something wrong with importing.

A second reason the idea is wrong is that it ignores the reality of commodity markets. It assumes we would weaken the oil-exporting countries we dislike if we stopped importing oil. The market for oil,

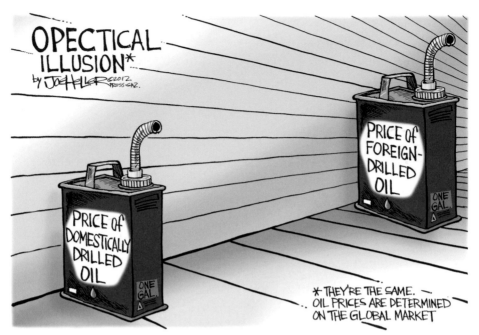

however, would simply absorb the U.S.'s foregone purchases. Any lowered demand might reduce the price of oil, and might reduce the overall volume annually purchased, but the lower price would encourage the use of oil by other consuming nations, and the lower volume of sales would just extend the number of years over which exporters would sell their oil. Further, any reduction in price or sales would affect all exporters, friends and foes.

## Oil Is a Rational Choice

A third reason the concept is wrong on its face is that it assumes the U.S. could, within economic reasonableness, become energy independent. Only the market can tell us what energy makes economic sense, and what commodities should be imported. The market informs us currently that oil and gas are economical sources of energy, and that we benefit from importing these. The alternative to allowing economic forces to guide us is to starve ourselves in service of myths.

Advocates of energy independence seek to moralize the issue by misleadingly referring to "our oil addiction." The use of a particular fuel is not an unhealthy compulsion, just a rational choice based on cost.

Advocates also refer to an "energy crisis." The only thing that could cause a crisis is the government's interference in the market, as by foolishly forcing the country to seek energy independence.

## Fears About Energy Dependence Are Misguided

The first problem with this concern is that it ignores the actual source of oil imports. As recently pointed out by Jerry Taylor of the Cato Institute, of the total of $188.5 billion of oil the U.S. imported in 2009, a fraction, $35.6 billion, came from the Middle East. Further, "only 15.5 percent of the oil in the world market is produced from nation-states accused of funding terrorism." In fact, Canada is the largest oil exporter to the U.S.

The second problem is that it assumes any income to hostile countries has a material effect on threats to the U.S. This is not the case. Terrorism is a low cost endeavor; even a significant decline in revenue would leave hostile countries billions to finance terrorism; and the level of terrorism does not correlate with the level of oil exports.

The third problem is that oil wealth is neither necessary nor sufficient to cause countries to act poorly towards their own people or other countries, and, again, bad behavior does not correlate with the level of exports.

As noted above, the exports of hostile or potentially hostile countries represent only a fraction of the U.S.'s oil imports. This itself should dampen fears of an embargo. The existence of the global oil market, however, moots the concern.

As discussed by [Jerry] Taylor and [Peter] Van Doren, an oil embargo against the U.S. would be ineffective because, once oil is in the market, any purchaser can access it. The authors note that the U.S.'s crude oil imports actually increased during the 1973 Arab embargo. They summarize: "In short, it does not matter to consumers to whom

> ## FAST FACT
>
> According to the American Council for an Energy-Efficient Economy, energy efficiency, rather than energy independence, should be the nation's goal. The council says that focusing on energy efficiency could reduce energy use by 40 to 60 percent by 2050.

*Although the 1973 Arab oil embargo caused long lines at gas stations, US oil imports actually increased.*

the oil is initially sold. All that matters to consumers is how much oil is produced for world markets."

## Alternative Sources of Energy Are Wasteful and Inferior

Some environmentalists use the energy independence argument to justify a transition away from imported oil towards alternative energy. "Alternative" invariably means "uneconomical;" otherwise the energy would be used without discussion. The proponents of alternative energy seek taxpayer subsidies and government-coerced use to make these fuels profitable for the suppliers.

A basic problem in government even getting involved in energy policy is that not only is it not omniscient, but it generally does what is in its own interest rather than the public interest. Government exploits economic myths to expand its power and favor special interests, and this is the case with alternative energy. Government's energy intervention is economically wasteful and environmentally counterproductive.

Consider government's promotion of ethanol and other biofuels in the name of alleged global warming. As discussed by Indur M. Goklany, such policies have caused crops to be diverted from food to fuel, and rainforest converted to agricultural land, increasing the problem of hunger and leading to ecological devastation. In fact, the agriculture needed to supply crops for biofuel itself leads to massive use of water and fertilizer, with negative environmental effects. Biofuels may even increase, rather than decrease, the emission of carbon dioxide.

The subsidies favor farming interests. The fact that the policies are designed to help these interests, rather than to provide environmental benefits, is reflected by the existence of protectionist tariffs on imported biofuels. If environmental concerns were the actual priority, government would welcome imports of biofuels.

## Energy Independence Should Not Be the Goal

Government uses not only environmental myths to promote alternative energy, but also economic myths. It takes advantage of people's concern with unemployment by falsely claiming it can create "green jobs."

The goal of seeking energy independence is fallacious. It is wrong on its face, and the justifications related to international relations, security, and environmental concerns are erroneous.

### EVALUATING THE AUTHOR'S ARGUMENTS:

Dave Shellenberger offers an uncommon perspective when he advises the United States not to become energy independent. How do you think the other authors in this chapter would respond to this provocative idea? For each author, write one to two sentences on how you think they would respond. Then, analyze the results—do any of the authors' positions surprise you? Why? In the end, do you think the United States should strive to become energy independent or not?

# Chapter 3

# What Energy Sources Might Replace Oil?

*Many believe that alternative energies such as wind and solar power can help alleviate US dependence on oil.*

# Nuclear Energy Can Replace Oil

*"If the hundred or so new nuclear plants previously proposed in China up to 2030 are not built, it is a fair bet that more than a billion tons can be added to annual global carbon dioxide emissions as a result."*

## Mark Lynas

In the following viewpoint Mark Lynas argues that nuclear power is the best alternative to oil. He discusses how in 2011 an offshore earthquake and tsunami destroyed parts of Japan, including a town that housed a nuclear power plant. Lynas admits this was a crisis but says the health threat to the general public was much lower than reported in the media. Despite this the crisis made countries wary about moving forward with their nuclear power programs, and many resumed burning oil, coal, and other fossil fuel energy sources. Lynas says this is an enormous mistake—using these fuels causes pollution and climate change, which puts the global population at much greater risk than it ever faced from the nuclear power accident. Lynas says nuclear power plants are continually being upgraded and made safer, so the risk of future accidents is small. He believes nuclear power can offer the world a cleaner, safer, and more responsible source of power than either oil or renewable resources like solar and wind. Lynas is the author of *Six Degrees: Our Future on a Hotter Planet* and *High Tide: The Truth About Our Climate Crisis*.

**AS YOU READ, CONSIDER THE FOLLOWING QUESTIONS:**
1. What does the phrase "making the perfect the enemy of the good" mean in the context of the viewpoint?
2. How many degrees warmer does the author say the planet will get if the world rejects nuclear power?
3. What is an "integral fast reactor" and how does it factor into the author's argument?

What a strange turn of events. Instead of uniting the environmental movement in renewed opposition to nuclear power, the Fukushima disaster in Japan[1] has divided it still further. An increasing number of green advocates, including some very prominent voices, have declared their support for nuclear power as a clean energy option, even as radioactive water accumulates and the timeline for cleaning up the contaminated areas extends by decades. Can they be serious?

They can. The irony of Fukushima is that in forcing us all to confront our deepest fears about the dangers of nuclear power, we find many of them to be wildly irrational—based on scare stories propagated through years of unchallenged mythology and the repeated exaggerations of self-proclaimed "experts" in the anti-nuclear movement. As the British environmental writer George Monbiot has pointed out, if we took the scientific consensus on nuclear energy as seriously as we take the scientific consensus on climate change, we environmentalists would be telling a very different story.

## Nuclear Fallout Was Not That Dangerous

The science on radiation tells us that the effects of Fukushima are serious but so far much less so than some of the more hyperbolic media coverage might suggest. The power plant operator, Tokyo Electric Power Co., has been releasing enormous quantities of radioactive water into the sea, for example. It sounds scary, but a member of the public would have to eat seaweed and seafood harvested just one mile from the discharge pipe for a year to receive an effective dose of 0.6

1. On March 11, 2011, an offshore earthquake triggered a tsunami that decimated parts of Japan. Damaged in the disaster was a nuclear power plant that released radioactive materials into the air.

millisieverts. To put this in context, every American receives on average 3 millisieverts each year from natural background radiation, and a hundred times more than this in some naturally radioactive areas. As for the Tokyo tap water that was declared unsafe for babies, the highest measured levels of radioactivity were 210 becquerels per liter, less than a quarter of the European legal limit of 1,000 becquerels per liter. Those leaving Tokyo because of this threat will have received more radiation on the airplane flight out than if they had been more rational and stayed put.

For the green movement, which is often justifiably accused of making the perfect the enemy of the good, having to confront real-world choices about energy technologies is painful. Most environmentalists assert that a combination of renewables and efficiency can decarbonize our energy

*Nuclear energy could be a viable alternative to oil and coal for generating electrical power. Nuclear power's downside, however, is the difficulty and danger of nuclear waste disposal.*

supply and save us both from global warming and the presumed dangers of nuclear power. This is technically possible but extremely unlikely in practice. In the messy real world, countries that decide to rely less on nuclear will almost certainly dig themselves even deeper into a dependence on dirty fossil fuels, especially coal.

## The Rush to Abandon Nuclear Power Imperils Us All

In the short term, this is already happening. In Germany—whose government tried to curry favor with a strongly anti-nuclear population by rashly closing seven perfectly safe nuclear plants after the Fukushima crisis began—coal has already become the dominant factor in electricity prices once again. Regarding carbon dioxide emissions, you can do the math: Just add about 11 million tons per year for each nuclear plant replaced by a coal plant newly built or brought back onto the grid.

In China the numbers become even starker. Coal is cheap there (as are the thousands of human lives lost in extracting it each year), and if the hundred or so new nuclear plants previously proposed in China up to 2030 are not built, it is a fair bet that more than a billion tons can be added to annual global carbon dioxide emissions as a result.

**FAST FACT**

According to the Nuclear Energy Institute, as of 2012 thirty countries were operating 436 nuclear reactors, which provided 13.5 percent of the world's electricity. France relies most heavily on nuclear energy, which supplies nearly 78 percent of that country's electricity.

Japan is also heavily dependent on coal, so it is a fair bet that less nuclear power there will add substantially to the country's emissions. No wonder the Japanese are insisting on backing off from the Kyoto climate treaty. Looking at the entire global picture, I estimate that turning away from nuclear power could make the difference between whether the world warms by 2 degrees Celsius (bad but manageable) and 3 degrees Celsius (disastrous) in the next century.

We have already made this mistake once. In the 1970s it looked as if nuclear power was going to play a much bigger role than eventually

# American Opinions About Nuclear Power

The majority of Americans think the country's existing nuclear power plants should remain open. They also would not want to pay the higher prices that would result from abandoning nuclear power as an energy source.

**Question: "Do you think any of the existing nuclear power plants in this country should be permanently shut down or do you think all of them should continue to operate?"**

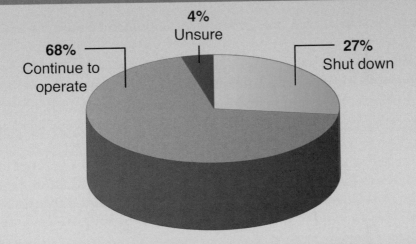

4%
Unsure

68%
Continue to
operate

27%
Shut down

**Question: "If the development of nuclear power were to be reduced in the immediate years ahead, . . . would you, yourself, be willing to pay higher prices for electricity in order to reduce the nation's dependency on nuclear power, or not?"**

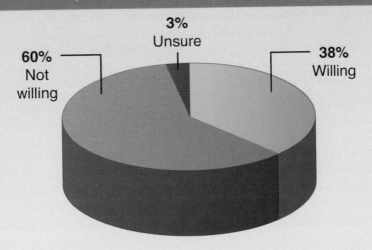

3%
Unsure

60%
Not
willing

38%
Willing

Taken from: CBS News poll. March 18–21, 2011; CNN/Opinion Research Corporation poll, March 18–20, 2011.

turned out to be the case. What happened was Three Mile Island, and the birth of an anti-nuclear movement that stopped dozens of half-built or proposed reactors; coal plants were substituted instead. It is therefore fair to say that the environmental movement played a substantial role in causing global warming, surely an ecological error it should learn from in years ahead.

## Nuclear Is the Best Alternative Energy

Don't get me wrong: I am an enthusiastic proponent of replacing fossil fuels with renewable energy sources. I strongly support wind, solar and other clean-tech options. But all energy technologies come with an ecological price tag. Wind turbines kill and injure birds and bats. Solar thermal plants proposed in the Mojave Desert have conservationists up in arms. If we are serious about taking biodiversity into consideration as well as climate change, these concerns cannot be idly dismissed. In terms of land use, nuclear scores very well, because the comparatively small quantities of fuel required means less land disturbed or ruined by mines, processing and related uses.

Take Japan again. According to some recent number crunching by the Breakthrough Institute, a centrist environmental think tank, phasing out Japan's current nuclear generation capacity and replacing it with wind would require a 1.3-million-acre wind farm, covering less than 3 percent of Japan's total land mass. Going for solar instead would require a similar land area, and would in economic terms cost the country more than a trillion dollars.

Those debating the future of nuclear power also tend to focus on out-of-date technology. No one proposes to build boiling-water reactors of 1960s-era Fukushima vintage in the 21st century. Newer designs have a much greater reliance on passive safety, as well as a host of other improvements. Fourth-generation options, such as the "integral fast reactor" [IFR] reportedly being considered by Russia, could be even better. Fast-breeders like the IFR will allow us to power whole countries cleanly by burning existing stockpiles of nuclear waste, depleted uranium and military-issue plutonium. And the waste left over at the end would become safe after a mere 300 years, so no Yucca Mountains[2] needed there. IFRs exist only on paper, however; we need to urgently research prototypes before moving on to large-scale deployment.

2. A controversial nuclear waste storage site proposed in Nevada.

## Even with Problems, Nuclear Power Is Better than Oil

What is needed is perspective. Nuclear energy is not entirely safe, as Fukushima clearly shows, even if the current radiation-related death toll is zero and will likely remain so. But coal and other fossil fuels are far, far worse. And insisting only on renewables risks worsening global warming as an unintended consequence. We need a portfolio of clean energy technologies, deployed in the most environmentally responsible way. Above all, let us base our energy policy on a scientifically valid appreciation of real-world risk, and not on scare stories from the past.

**EVALUATING THE AUTHOR'S ARGUMENTS:**

In this viewpoint Mark Lynas uses facts, statistics, examples, and reasoning to make his argument that nuclear power is safe and efficient. He does not, however, use any quotations to support his point. If you were to rewrite this article and insert quotations, what authorities might you quote from? Where would you place quotations, and why?

# Nuclear Energy Is Not a Good Alternative to Oil

**Veronique de Rugy**

*"More nuclear won't mean less oil."*

In the following viewpoint Veronique de Rugy argues that nuclear power is not a good replacement for oil. She explains that nuclear power remains very expensive—it is several times more expensive to generate than fossil fuels like oil, gas, and coal. The true cost of nuclear power is even higher, explains de Rugy, who says its price is artificially brought down by tax breaks and financial incentives given to nuclear power plants by governments. Most importantly, de Rugy says using nuclear power would not put a dent in the amount of oil Americans use. She explains that nuclear power is mostly used to generate electricity; but oil would still be needed for transportation and to make products. For all of these reasons, she concludes that nuclear power will never replace oil. De Rugy is a senior research fellow at the Mercatus Center at George Mason University. She writes and testifies before Congress on issues relating to the US economy, homeland security, taxation, and energy.

**AS YOU READ, CONSIDER THE FOLLOWING QUESTIONS:**
  1. How much more does nuclear-powered energy cost per unit of electricity than gas, according to the author?
  2. What is a subsidy and how does it factor into the author's argument?
  3. What does de Rugy say nuclear power is primarily used for? What about oil? What bearing does this have on her argument?

As Jerry Taylor of the Cato Institute wrote in *Reason* magazine in 2009, "Nuclear energy is to the Right what solar energy is to the Left: Religious devotion in practice, a wonderful technology in theory, but an economic white elephant in fact (some crossovers on both sides notwithstanding). When the day comes that the electricity from solar or nuclear power plants is worth more than the costs associated with generating it, I will be as happy . . . to support either technology."

Until that time comes, producing nuclear energy remains a very costly business.

## Nuclear Power Is Very Expensive

A 2009 interdisciplinary study at the Massachusetts Institute of Technology compare[d] the costs of generating a kilowatt hour of electricity using nuclear, coal, and gas power. Looking at this data, the cost differential is clear—nuclear-powered energy costs 14 percent more than gas to produce a unit of electricity, and it costs 30 percent more than coal. Furthermore, according to Gilbert Metcalf's [September 2009] National Bureau of Economic Research paper on energy, this increased cost of nuclear energy includes a baked-in taxpayer subsidy of nearly 50 percent of nuclear power's operating costs.

While the nuclear industry in the United States has seen continued improvements in operating performance over time, it remains uncompetitive with coal and natural gas on the basis of price. This cost differential is primarily the result of high capital costs and long construction times. Indeed, building a nuclear power plant in the United States has cost, on average, three times as [much as] was originally estimated.

The United States Energy Information Administration estimates that these cost trends will continue for the near future. . . .

Nuclear power remains more expensive than other conventional forms of power.

As Taylor notes, this is why nuclear power has only flourished in countries where the government has intervened on its behalf. . . .

## Nuclear Power Only Works When Heavily Supported by Governments

Many Americans argue that government regulations are the real reason why nuclear power is so expensive. As evidence, they point out that in France, where there is more opportunity to build nuclear power plants, nuclear power is safe and affordable.

It is true that France gets about 75 percent of its electricity from nuclear power. It is also true that the country has avoided a large-scale disaster due to the many safety regulations it has imposed, most of which are similar to regulations enacted in the U.S.

However, producing nuclear energy in France is not any cheaper than it is here. . . . In U.S. dollars, the parity between the costs of generating nuclear power in the United States (which has a relatively strict regulatory regime) and France (which has a relatively loose one).

A range of estimates of the costs of nuclear reactors in the two countries [has been] gathered by Mark Cooper, a senior research fellow for economic analysis at the Institute for Energy and the Environment at the Vermont Law School. As Cooper found, the ranges overlap: France's estimated cost of a kilowatt of power is between $4,500 and $5,000; the United States' estimated cost for this unit of power is between $4,000 and $6,000.

## "A Poor Investment"

From the start of commercial nuclear reactor construction in the mid-1960s through the 1980s, capital costs (dollars per kilowatt of capacity) for building nuclear reactors rose dramatically. Although unit costs for technology usually decrease with volume of production because of scale factors and technological learning, nuclear power has gone in the opposite direction. This exception to the rule is usu-

## More Nuclear Might Not Mean Less Oil

Oil provides a tiny amount of American electricity, and nuclear power largely generates electricity. Therefore, some experts claim that increasing nuclear power use will have no effect on the amount of oil that is used.

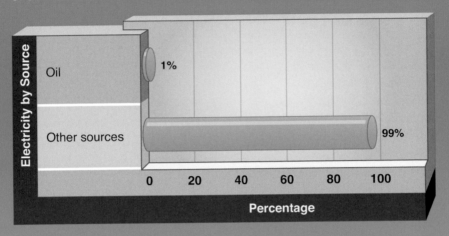

Taken from: US Energy Information Administration, 2010.

ally attributed to the idiosyncrasies of the nuclear regulatory environment as public opposition grew, laws were tightened, and construction times increased.

As a result, no new nuclear power plants have been built in the United States in 29 years. Nuclear has proven to be a poor investment, producing far more expensive electricity than originally promised. . . .

## Using Nuclear Power Would Not Reduce the Need for Oil

On last Sunday's [March 20, 2011,] *Meet the Press*, Sen. Charles Schumer (D-NY) cited America's need to get off of foreign oil as a strong reason for pursuing nuclear power.

Setting aside the misguided goal of so-called energy independence, Schumer is still wrong. Oil is primarily used in vehicles and in industrial production. Nuclear power is primarily used for electricity.

Data from the United States Energy Information Administration shows that the vast majority of our electricity comes from non-oil sources.

Interestingly, according to Michael Levi, a senior fellow and director of the program on energy security and climate change at the Council on Foreign Relations, it wasn't always the case. "During the heyday of nuclear power, the early 1970s (45 plants broke ground between 1970 and 1975)," Levi writes, "oil was a big electricity source, and boosting nuclear power was a real way to squeeze petroleum out of the economy. Alas, we've already replaced pretty much all the petroleum in the power sector; the opportunity to substitute oil with nuclear power is gone."

Perhaps more importantly, less than 1 percent of the oil used in the United States today goes to generate electricity while 70 percent is consumed by the transportation sector, with roughly 30 percent of oil being used by the residential and industrial sectors.

The bottom line is that more nuclear power would mean less coal, less natural gas, less hydroelectric power, and less wind energy. But more nuclear won't mean less oil.

## Nuclear Power Can Never Be Sustainable

Am I against nuclear power? It certainly looks like nuclear can never be a sustainable source of energy because it is just too expensive. And while it is a safe source of energy overall, there are tremendous risks in those instances where something goes disastrously wrong. The probability of such a dire scenario may be low, but the need to build in protections against it will always raise the cost of producing nuclear power.

But more importantly, what I am against is the government deciding that nuclear power must be encouraged and then subsidizing

*A nuclear power plant in France generates electricity. The cost of building a reactor for France's mostly nuclear-powered grid is estimated at $4,500 to $5,000 per kilowatt of power capacity while the United States' cost for its nuclear-powered plants is about the same. World reactor capacities may vary from, for example, 300 to 1600 megawatts.*

the industry. On that point, I leave the last word to *Reason* Science Correspondent Ronald Bailey.

"The main problem with energy supply systems is that for the last 100 years, governments have insisted on meddling with them, using subsidies, setting rates, and picking technologies," Bailey observes. "Consequently, entrepreneurs, consumers, and especially policymakers have no idea which power supply technologies actually provide the best balance between cost-effectiveness and safety. In any case, let's hope that the current nuclear disaster will not substantially add to the terrible woes the Japanese must bear as a result of nature's fickle cruelty."

## EVALUATING THE AUTHOR'S ARGUMENTS:

A main element of de Rugy's argument is that nuclear energy cannot be used for vehicles or creating products, and so it will not reduce oil use. Research this claim. Is de Rugy correct? Is nuclear power use irrelevant to oil use? Why or why not? Be sure to cite the sources you used in your research.

# Renewable Resources Can Replace Oil

**Chris Williams**

*"It is fully within our means today to make the alternative energy dream a green reality."*

Clean, renewable energy can replace oil, argues Chris Williams in the following viewpoint. He discusses how the planet generates an enormous amount of renewable energy each day. Harvesting this energy requires building infrastructure, a new energy grid, and things like wind turbines and solar panels, but Williams argues once these systems are in place, humans will have more clean energy than they could ever possibly use. Using a mix of renewable energy sources will ensure that power is available all the time, he says, and these energy sources will be conflict-free and less prone to disasters or accidents. The environmental, economic, health, and safety benefits of using renewable energy are numerous, concludes Williams—the only thing holding civilization back from making this great leap are politics and lack of imagination. Williams is a professor of physics and chemistry at Pace University. He is the author of *Ecology and Socialism: Solutions to Capitalist Ecological Crises.*

Chris Williams, "How to Green the Planet," *Indypendent*, no. 166, June 10, 2011.

**AS YOU READ, CONSIDER THE FOLLOWING QUESTIONS:**
1. What portion of incoming solar radiation does Williams say would need to be captured to meet all of humanity's energy needs?
2. How much wind energy is available in the United States, according to Williams?
3. How many cars are manufactured each year? How does this factor into the author's argument?

I
t may seem hard to believe, but it is fully within our means today to make the alternative energy dream a green reality. All the technologies exist. The engineering is relatively straightforward, especially when compared to the epic size of our oil-powered, automobile-based societies. The need is obvious. Unless we want to consign humanity to a broiling, toxic swamp called earth, alternative energy is an imperative.

The tricky part, however, is society and politics. How our society and economy is organized; how wealth and resources are generated and distributed; which institutions have a vested interest in the status quo; and how to create radically different forms of decision making are the major obstacles to greening the global economy.

The first question is, are there even enough alternative sources of energy to harvest? Different studies provide the answer.

## Renewable Energy Is Unbelievably Plentiful

Last August [2010], *Science Magazine* reported that 101,000 terawatts of solar energy strikes the ground each year. This compares to annual global energy consumption of 15 terawatts for everything: heating, electricity and transport. (One terawatt is a million megawatts, roughly equivalent to the output of 1,200 nuclear power reactors.) Therefore, we only have to capture a little more than 1/10,000th of incoming solar radiation to satisfy all of humanity's energy needs.

Wind energy is not so abundant, but still plentiful. A recent report by the National Renewable Energy Laboratory put the total wind energy available in the United States at 37,000,000 gigawatt-hours of electricity, which is 12 times the demand. A 2005 study by Stanford

University researchers found worldwide 72 terawatts of "sustainable class 3 winds," meaning they are highly efficient for generating electricity. This estimate, which researchers call conservative, is nearly five time global energy demand.

A comprehensive 2006 report by MIT, "The Future of Geothermal Energy," estimated that if the United States accessed just 2 percent of its geothermal potential, it would amount to 280 times our entire annual consumption. One recent study carried out at Stanford detailed how 100 percent of California's energy needs could be reliably met by 2020 with a mix of geothermal, solar and wind power alongside existing hydroelectricity.

## There Is More than Enough to Go Around

The October 2009 issue of *Scientific American* featured another study detailing how to generate 100 percent of the world's energy from renewable sources by 2030. It would require manufacturing 3.8 million large wind turbines and 90,000 solar plants, and deploying geothermal, tidal and rooftop photovoltaic installations. The cost estimate was significantly less than if the same power was generated via fossil fuels and nuclear power. The construction of 3.8 million wind turbines might sound like a lot over a 20-year period but as 70 million cars are manufactured every year, it is very feasible.

Clearly, the amount of energy available from solar, wind and geothermal sources, even without adding in tidal and wave energy, dwarfs current and foreseeable demand. . . .

## We Can Harness the Sun and Wind

Renewable energy sources are supposedly too diffuse to capture efficiently, even if it's technically free. Skeptics claim huge swaths of land would be gobbled up by the wind turbines and solar arrays needed to replace coal, oil and nuclear power. This raises another problem: the overall cost to build and maintain the new infrastructure and the resources required to do so.

At least in the United States, dispersion is not an issue. High-quality wind power is abundant in the Great Plains and Texas and along the Eastern seaboard. The Southwest is bathed in sunshine that can be efficiently collected. A considerable amount of space would have to

*A wind power plant is under construction. Alternative energy will require building a new infrastructure, a new energy grid to distribute the power generated by wind and solar power plants.*

be devoted to turbines, solar plants and the storage, transmission and distribution grid. But these would be located in sparsely populated areas, and would take up far less space than the existing infrastructure for oil, coal, natural gas and nuclear power, without even including all the waste dumps and poisoned lands.

## How to Deal with Dark, Windless Days

The second argument against renewables is because the sun and wind are somewhat unpredictable, we need carbon-based or nuclear power systems to smooth out fluctuations in supply or to account for demand spikes. Built-in redundancy to account for this problem is prohibitive in terms of cost, land and resource use.

The intermittency problem can be solved with a mix of renewables. First, wind and solar energy complement one another: wind is more prevalent and predictable at night, while solar is obviously limited to the day. Geothermal energy is highly predictable, as is tidal and wave-based energy. Second, if the mix of renewables is spread geographically, then there is a high probability that energy will be reliably available.

Third, to iron out any spikes, an electrical system based on renewable energy would require storage rather than redundancy—which in any case is already required with fossil fuel and nuclear plants. There are a number of proven technologies that can be used to store electricity. Solar energy can be stored for nighttime use by heating up salts during the day. And solar or wind power can [be] stored by compressing air, pumping water uphill, or by employing flywheels.

## The Way Forward

To make this system viable electricity grids must be upgraded. In the United States, the antiquated grid is a hodgepodge of three semi-autonomous regions with little interconnectivity and a morass of smaller lines zigzagging haphazardly across states. These grids are prone to costly accidents, power shortages and blackouts. High voltage power lines take up less land than those currently in use and are more efficient. Incorporating some high-voltage direct current lines—which lose far less electricity in long-distance transmission than alternating current lines—would also reduce energy usage.

Such a project would require federal intervention. However, when one looks at the interstate highway system—a huge subsidy to the auto industry—building a national super highway for clean-energy electrons is hardly unprecedented.

A 2009 publication, "Energy Self-Reliant States," found that 30 states could be entirely self-sufficient in energy without requiring long-distance power transmission. Therefore, a mix of decentralized and centralized energy is entirely possible.

## A Cleaner, Safer Planet

Other advantages of renewable energy over fossil fuels and nuclear power include greatly reducing the possibility of breathing poisoned air, drinking polluted water and living on an irradiated and dying planet. Also, contrary to prevailing belief, wind turbines and solar photovoltaic panels require far less downtime for maintenance than fossil-fuel or nuclear power plants. As renewables are dispersed by nature and most will not be grouped in massive gigawatt-sized plants, taking turbines or solar panels offline is much less disruptive than shutting down just one large coal-fired power plant. Out of the more than 1,000 wind turbines operating in Japan, only one was damaged by the earthquake and ensuing tsunami. Therefore, resilience to natural disasters is another bonus of renewable energy sources.

One of the most intriguing benefits of renewable energies is that energy consumption would drop dramatically. According to *Scientific American*, "electrification is a more efficient way to use energy. For example, only 17 to 20 percent of the energy in gasoline is used to move a vehicle (the rest is wasted as heat), whereas 75 to 86 percent of the electricity delivered to an electric vehicle goes into motion."

## Renewables Are Comparable in Price

Perhaps the most-common argument leveled against renewable is its expense. Nuclear-power proponents claim it is the cheapest form of energy per kilowatt-hour, less expensive than coal, oil or wind. This is true, if one ignores decommissioning costs for hundreds of nuclear reactors, the hundreds of billions of dollars that it will cost to handle

# Americans Want to Pursue Alternative Energies

Multiple polls taken in 2012 revealed that the majority of Americans think it is more important to develop alternative energy sources like wind and solar power than it is to pursue fossil fuels like oil.

Question: "Which of the following approaches to solving the nation's energy problems do you think the US should follow right now: emphasize production of more oil, gas and coal supplies, or emphasize the development of alternative energy such as wind and solar power?"

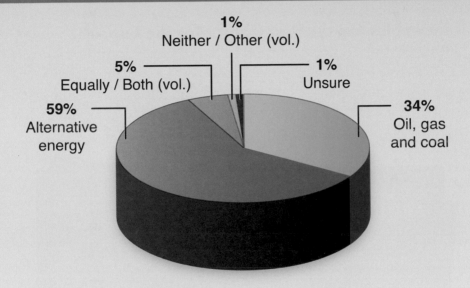

1%
Neither / Other (vol.)

5%
Equally / Both (vol.)

1%
Unsure

59%
Alternative
energy

34%
Oil, gas
and coal

Taken from: Gallup poll, March 8–11, 2012; Pew Research Center survey, March 7–11, 2012.

the Fukushima disaster over the next 100 years, lands devastated by uranium mining, at least 150,000 deaths from the 1986 meltdown at Chernobyl, and tens of thousands of years of continuing poisoning from highly radioactive waste that no one has a clue what to do with. Wind is already cheaper than natural gas and coal, with almost none of the environmental drawbacks, from mining and fracking to acid rain and climate change.

According to the winter 2011 issue of *Good* magazine, U.S. government subsidies to the fossil fuel industry in the form of tax breaks and direct spending totaled $70.2 billion from 2002 to 2008. Corn-based ethanol received $16.8 billion more while all other renewable technologies received only $12.2 billion.

Globally, price and production incentives for fossil fuels was an eye-popping $650 billion in 2008; this for the most profitable industry on the planet. Exxon Mobil alone reaped $30.5 billion in profit for 2010.

As for investments in green energy, [in 2010] the United States spent $18 billion while China allocated $34 billion. China and South Korea far exceed the United States in the manufacture and production of green technology and will move further ahead over the next several years as public funding increases. . . .

## Renewables Are the Best Choice for the Future

Ultimately, we need a revolution in social power in order to create a sustainable world based on clean power. Under a different social system, one not predicated on profit-taking, but one based on cooperation, real democracy and production for need, we can finally live sustainably with the planet on which we depend.

> **EVALUATING THE AUTHOR'S ARGUMENTS:**
>
> To support their arguments, Chris Williams and Dana Joel Gattuso, author of the following viewpoint, rely on facts and statistics from numerous sources. Catalog each of their facts and statistics. What specific points do they support? Are they taken from credible, authoritative sources? Make a chart that shows which information is taken from which sources, and what arguments the information specifically supports. Then state which author you think used better sources and made the better argument.

**Viewpoint**

**4**

# Renewable Resources Cannot Replace Oil

## Dana Joel Gattuso

*"The main reason renewables will not be a prominent provider of energy is that they simply do not produce enough energy output."*

Dana Joel Gattuso is a senior fellow in environmental policy at the National Center for Public Policy Research. In the following viewpoint she argues that renewable resources are not environmentally friendly and will never be able to replace oil. Renewable resources like wind and solar power are very expensive to produce, she explains. They are also unreliable because they are unable to provide power when the sun does not shine or the wind does not blow. We lack the technology to harness enough wind or sun to transform them into a usable energy source, and doing so will take generations and destroy the environment, she claims. All of these reasons are why renewables continue to account for a small portion of US energy, says Gattuso. She concludes that renewables will never be cost-effective, powerful, or environmentally friendly enough to replace oil as an energy source.

AS YOU READ, CONSIDER THE FOLLOWING QUESTIONS:
  1. How much does wind energy cost per kilowatt-hour, according to Gattuso?
  2. About what percentage of Americans' total energy comes from renewable energy, according to Gattuso?
  3. What effect would the installation of solar panels have on wild spaces in California and Nevada, according to Gattuso?

Renewable energy is a scarce resource, extremely costly, and will impose a heavy tax burden on consumers and the economy. The following debunks just some of the myths over renewable energy sources. . . .

## There Is Nothing Cheap About Renewable Energy

Wind and sunshine may seem like free and plentiful sources of energy. Yet there is nothing cheap about renewable energy. The costs of producing and transmitting alternative sources are astronomical. Even after the federal government has provided billions of tax dollars in support over the past three decades to bring the price down on renewables, their costs soar high above fossil fuel energy sources.

Most estimates put the cost of wind energy at more than 50 percent over the cost of energy from coal. According to a recent study by Black & Veatch, a Kansas-based company that builds coal, gas, and wind plants, wind power costs more than 12 cents per kilowatt-hour—the cost of getting a kilowatt of power for an hour—while energy from coal plants costs about 7.8 cents per kilowatt-hour.

## Renewable Energy Is Unreliable

One of the reasons wind is so costly is that it is unreliable. Even the windiest areas of the nation cannot rely on a continuous supply of wind and need backup plants generated by natural gas to take over when [the] wind fails. That adds significantly to the cost.

Even with President [Barack] Obama's stimulus package providing over $10 billion to jurisdictions that "go green," local governments are finding the costs of renewable power are simply too high. The city of Durango, Colorado has powered its government buildings for two years [since 2007] by purchasing electricity from nearby wind farms. It now finds it can no longer afford producing wind power and will save the city $45,000 by reverting back to coal-fired electricity. According to the city manager, "It's very hard for us to lay off an employee to justify green power. Those are the trade-offs you have to face."

Wind power companies say their customers will have to get used to paying higher utility bills to support their industry, according to *Greenwire*. As the chief officer of the company First Wind said at an investors meeting, "The key is the regulators and customers need to be willing to pay the higher prices. What you're betting on is the increasing demand for renewable energy."

Solar power is even more expensive, costing 20 to 40 cents per kilowatt-hour, compared to about 8 cents from coal. . . .

## A Fraction of All Energy Use

Even after accounting for President Obama's ambitious and costly stimulus plan to ratchet up federal spending for alternative energy by $100 billion, renewables will still comprise a small amount of all energy use.

Although the federal government has supported and subsidized renewable energy for a quarter century, renewables still remain a small portion—8 percent—of the total energy that Americans consume. Corn-based ethanol makes up most of the share of renewable energy. Wind and solar generation are miniscule, only a fraction of a percent of all energy use. Although demand for wind power has been on the rise the past few years, the U.S.'s electricity still overwhelmingly comes from hydrocarbons—primarily coal (49 percent) and natural gas (21 percent). . . .

The main reason renewables will not be a prominent provider of energy is that they simply do not produce enough energy output. Take wind power. By 2010, some experts project wind turbines in the United States will produce an annual 112 billion kilowatt-hours of energy. That may sound like a lot but Robert Bryce, author of *Gusher of Lies*, puts that number in perspective by pointing out that in 2006, U.S. consumer electronics alone generated 147 billion kilowatt-hours of electricity. Or that the nation's coal-fired plants generate over 2,022 billion kilowatt-hours of power a year.

Moreover, while wind capacity has been rising in the last few years due to massive infusion of government support and subsidies, it is expected to actually fall this year [2009] for the first time since 2004, according to the American Wind Energy Association, reflecting wind's inability to compete in price with natural gas. Its faltering track-record has prompted [entrepreneur] T. Boone Pickens to scrap his $10 billion wind power project announced in 2007 to create the world's most massive wind farm in the Texas Panhandle.

## The Technology Does Not Exist

The fact remains that the economics and technology for a shift in the next few decades from fossil fuels to wind and solar is simply not there. President Obama's secretary of energy, Nobel Laureate Steven Chu, told the *New York Times* nothing short of a technological "revolution" is needed to make solar power happen, and that technology will have to get five times better than it currently is to have any impact in curtailing carbon dioxide emissions.

In California, where the wind blows and sun shines more than most states, power companies face a daunting mandate from Governor [Arnold] Schwarzenegger (R) to provide 33 percent renewables in the energy mix by 2020. Even providers in the renewable industry are dubious. CEO of Greenvolts, a California-based solar power company: "I think it's a huge challenge. I think it's going to take us a great effort from all different parts of industry and government to pull off. The grid that we need is not in place. The technologies are not in place." Others worry about the cost of the mandate.

Even European nations—which have struggled for decades to make renewables viable and are required by the European Union to bring these sources to 20 percent of energy use by 2020—have failed to make renew-

> **FAST FACT**
>
> *Forbes* magazine reports that in order to generate the amount of electricity provided by Phoenix's Palo Verde Nuclear Power Station, an area ten times larger than Washington, DC, would need to be paved with solar panels. It would also cost fifteen times more per kilowatt-hour.

# Renewable Energy Is a Small Slice of the Energy Pie

Together, renewable sources of energy account for a very small portion of energy. Opponents say this is because they are too expensive and do not generate significant amounts of power.

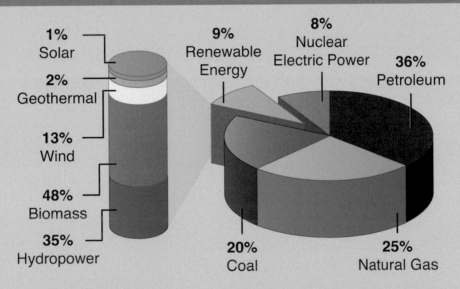

**US Energy Consumption by Energy Source, 2011**

1%
Solar

2%
Geothermal

13%
Wind

48%
Biomass

35%
Hydropower

9%
Renewable
Energy

8%
Nuclear
Electric Power

36%
Petroleum

20%
Coal

25%
Natural Gas

**Total: 9 quadrillion BTU**

**Total: 97.5 quadrillion BTU**

Taken from: US Energy Information Administration. *Monthly Energy Review*, Table 10.1, March 2012.

able energy part of the mainstream. Today renewables make up only 6 percent of total energy sources, little changed from a decade ago. . . .

## Renewable Energy Is Bad for the Environment

Increasingly, scientific, peer-reviewed studies are showing that the renewable energy sources being mandated by the Obama Administration and Congress would be extremely harmful to the environment and natural resources, and emit much larger amounts of carbon than fossil fuels. . . .

Solar and wind power . . . are embroiled in environmental battles, as Washington and the states move forward to mandate production, raising concerns about the impact that will have on protected lands and endangered species. The *New York Times*: There is an "emerging conflict between the Obama administration's plans to greatly expand the use of renewable energy and the concerns of those who fear solar arrays, wind farms and geothermal plants could disrupt or destroy wildlife habitat and soak up precious water supplies in the arid West."

To provide solar power of the magnitude that President Obama, Governor Schwarzenegger, and other lawmakers desire, millions of

*Most estimates put the cost of generating electricity from wind power at more than 50 percent higher than producing electricity from coal.*

acres would need to be cleared to install solar panels. In California and Nevada, environmentalists are battling officials over 160,000 acres of federal land in the Mojave Desert where they assert desert plants, endangered species, and water supplies are threatened by a wide expanse of large-scale solar installations.

## Paving Our Parks with Panels and Turbines

Sixty-three solar projects have been proposed for construction in the area on lands operated by the federal Bureau of Land Management. The National Park Service has warned the agency that "the projects could produce air and light pollution, generate noise and destroy wildlife habitat . . ." and "strain limited water resources already under pressure" from development.

Wind power also is under intense scrutiny for its impact on birds and other species on the endangered list, land use issues—powering New York City alone would require a wind farm covering an expanse the size of Connecticut—and, indirectly, carbon release.

Wind's variability requires that conventional power sources such as natural gas supplement wind farms. But greater reliance on natural gas than previously thought would result in higher levels of carbon emissions than has been reported. A study conducted by the Renewable Energy Foundation, a research organization in Great Britain, finds that in January, Great Britain's coldest month of the year and when energy demand is at its highest, wind capacity would not be high enough. Wind farms would be able to supply only four percent of their capacity, requiring fossil fuel plants to supplement power as often as 23 times a month, "impair[ing] efficiency and reduc[ing] emissions savings."

According to the researchers, "Carbon savings will be less than expected, because cheaper, less efficient plants will be used to support these wind power fluctuations. Neither these extra costs nor the increased carbon production are being taken into account in the government figures for wind power."

## A Lose-Lose Proposition

Detrimental to the environment in numerous respects, renewable energy fails to be the "green" environmentally-friendly alternative supporters promised it to be. Furthermore, renewables will impose enormous costs on consumers that even their proponents concede is a troublesome aspect of solar, wind, and biofuels. Renewable energy is a lose-lose proposition.

**EVALUATING THE AUTHOR'S ARGUMENTS:**

In this viewpoint Dana Joel Gattuso suggests that one problem with renewable resources is that they fail to provide power when the sun is not shining or the wind is not blowing. How might Chris Williams, author of the previous viewpoint, respond to this claim? After considering both positions, which do you think is correct, and why?

# Electric Cars Can Replace Oil-Fueled Ones

*"If the U.S. wants energy independence and doesn't want to cede its role as technology leader of the future, the rapid development and deployment of the electric car . . . should be a national priority."*

### Sarah A.W. Fitts

Electric cars are the vehicles of the future, argues Sarah A.W. Fitts in the following viewpoint. She is excited that electric vehicles are already available on the market and says they perform excellently. All they need, in her opinion, is more support from society and the government to make them more socially acceptable and convenient. Fitts believes transitioning to an electric fleet of vehicles will help save the environment and money, and it will help the United States avoid other problems that are associated with oil. She warns that if the country does not develop electric car technology, other countries will, and the United States will be left behind in the energy revolution of the future. Fitts is a lawyer who cochairs the Energy & Natural Resources Practice group at the New York law firm Debevoise & Plimpton.

**AS YOU READ, CONSIDER THE FOLLOWING QUESTIONS:**
1. What countries does Fitts worry are ahead of the United States in developing electric car technology?
2. How much per gallon does Fitts say it costs to operate an electric car?
3. What does the phrase "Sputnik Moment" mean in the context of the viewpoint?

What if you had the solution for the United States' dependence on imported oil parked in your garage? Elected officials and wanna-be-elected presidential candidates lament the dependence on imported oil, the price of gasoline and the alleged costs of subsidizing the clean tech industries, but the solutions they propose remain mid-twentieth century: more oil drilling, maintaining subsidies and other benefits for oil and gas producers, pipelines across irreplaceable farmland and aquifers, and rolling back environmental regulations that protect health and safety to reduce costs. Meanwhile, programs to promote the twenty-first century solutions, such as the electric car and other advanced technology vehicles, have been targeted for dramatic cuts in the latest round of budget fights.

## The Way to Keep America's Cars

The facts are straight-forward and compelling, and if they were better understood, the push for wide-spread development and adoption of the electric car and other alternate fuel vehicles would be bi-partisan and not controversial. The simple logic is this: the United States spends billions of dollars per month buying oil, much of it from regimes we do not consider to be our friends. Roughly two-thirds of the oil used in the United States is used in transportation. Almost no electricity in the United States is generated from oil. Therefore, by shifting transportation from gasoline to electric power we can give up oil without giving up our cars. That is why organizations like Securing America's Future Energy and its affiliate the Electrification Coalition, an organization supported and led by serious U.S. multinationals such as FedEx, are championing the electric car. It may be the simplest and most cost effective way to reduce our dependence on imported oil.

## Electric Cars Are Good for America

The global competition to develop the best batteries and electric car technologies is off and running. China, Korea, Japan and others are all making significant investments in developing the technology and manufacturing capacity. The United States, through the Department of Energy's Advanced Technology Vehicle Manufacturing Incentive Program has made loans to companies like Ford, Fisker, Tesla and Nissan to increase battery and advanced technology vehicle component manufacturing in the United States. Vehicle manufacturing in the United States is not just about creating jobs. It is about nurturing and growing an entire industry that starts with intellectual property,

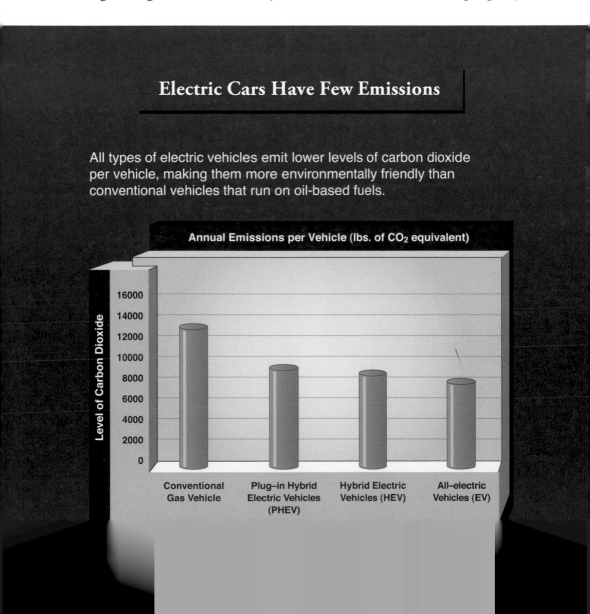

### Electric Cars Have Few Emissions

All types of electric vehicles emit lower levels of carbon dioxide per vehicle, making them more environmentally friendly than conventional vehicles that run on oil-based fuels.

**Annual Emissions per Vehicle (lbs. of $CO_2$ equivalent)**

including patents, know how, skills and includes the supply chain necessary to carry out the rapid innovation in this field. If next generation transportation is not developed here, it will surely be developed elsewhere, probably with assistance from other governments that want to build an industrial backbone, as we continue to allow ours to atrophy.

## Road-Ready and Real

The electric car is not pie in the sky. The electric car is real and you could buy one. The Chevy Volt is already available in dealerships near you. Other cars are on their way. Some are new American car companies: Tesla or Fisker. Others are names you already know: Ford and Nissan, for example. These are large companies that are making a significant bet on technology.

The electric car has some attractive advantages in its own right. First, we already have a fuel distribution system—every garage with an electric outlet could become a "filling station" every time a car is plugged in. Electric vehicles have limited or no tail pipe emissions, which could have significant positive benefits in congested areas. (The total air quality improvements, including green house gasses, will, obviously depend on what fuels are used to generate electricity, which is a separate but worthwhile discussion.) Finally, the cost of operating an electric car may be much cheaper than buying gasoline. FedEx's Gina Adams, in a keynote address at the RETECH 2011 conference in Washington, DC in September [2011], reported that FedEx operates vehicles in its electric fleet at the equivalent of 50¢ per gallon. If the front-end price can be reduced, the lifetime cost of car ownership could drop meaningfully.

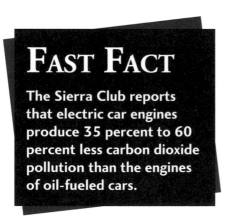

**FAST FACT**

The Sierra Club reports that electric car engines produce 35 percent to 60 percent less carbon dioxide pollution than the engines of oil-fueled cars.

## Challenges Can Be Overcome

The electric car has its skeptics, and appropriately so. The models currently available have range limitations and cannot be charged

*An electric car recharges at a recharging station. Many think electric cars will eventually replace gasoline-powered cars.*

fast enough to suit the needs of some drivers. In many parts of the country, the electric grid is decades old and some worry that it is not capable of serving the increased usage demands of electric cars. Electric cars remain expensive, relative to other cars, and reliability and maintenance are untested. And some people simply have a hard time imagining a car not run on gasoline. These are challenges that the car manufacturers and electric utilities will need to address to sell their products.

The twenty-first century car is electric. If the U.S. wants energy independence and doesn't want to cede its role as technology leader of the future, the rapid development and deployment of the electric car, and other alternate fuel vehicles, should be a national priority. As President [Barack] Obama and Department of Energy's Secretary [Steven] Chu have said, "This is Our Generation's Sputnik Moment".

The administration's push for wider investment in and adoption of energy efficient "green" technologies, including the electric car, should be a bipartisan effort.

## The Car of the Future Is Electric

Contact your representatives and let them know that you want America to be energy independent, that you want to drive the car of the future and that you want that car to be developed and made in America. It would be a sad day for the United States if the only way to reduce our dangerous and expensive dependence on imported oil is to replace it with a possibly dangerous and equally expensive dependence on imported batteries and electric drive components.

**EVALUATING THE AUTHOR'S ARGUMENTS:**

In this viewpoint Sarah A.W. Fitts uses reasoning, logic, examples, and information to argue that electric cars should be the car of the future. However, she uses very few facts or statistics to support her argument. Using your school library or the Internet, find at least two additional facts or statistics that could be used to support her work. These could be the results of an opinion poll, government study, or demographic survey. Make sure the source from which the fact or statistic comes is authoritative and credible.

**Viewpoint 6**

# Electric Cars Will Never Replace Oil-Fueled Ones

*"Upon closer consideration, shifting from gasoline to electric vehicles starts to appear synonymous with switching a smoking habit from cloves to menthols."*

## Ozzie Zehner

There are many critical problems with electric vehicles, argues Ozzie Zehner in the following viewpoint. He says that electric cars are not as clean as they are cracked up to be—they minimally reduce carbon dioxide emissions and are responsible for different kinds of environmental damage, such as that caused by mining metals for batteries. Their cost-efficiency, too, has been exaggerated. Zehner says that electric cars' expensive batteries cost owners much more in the long run than they would save on gas. In addition, because they are cars, they perpetuate a sprawling and wasteful lifestyle that Zehner says contributes to other kinds of environmental harm. For all of these reasons, he views electric cars as very similar to their oil-fueled counterparts and does not consider them to be a good replacement. Zehner is the author of *Green Illusions: The Dirty Secrets of Clean Energy and the Future of Environmentalism.*

**AS YOU READ, CONSIDER THE FOLLOWING QUESTIONS:**
1. What does Zehner say the Royal Society of Chemistry conclud-
   ed about electric cars' effect on Britain's total carbon dioxide
   emissions?
2. What piece of equipment critical to electric cars does Zehner say
   is typically left out of their price?
3. What did the National Academies conclude about environmental damage caused by mining materials for electric car batteries?

California passed a ruling on Jan. 27 [2012] requiring that
15 percent of new cars sold in the state meet a strict emissions standard of zero to near-zero emissions by 2015. Many
environmental groups are praising the decision, which will require
Californians to buy more electric, hybrid, and hydrogen vehicles. I
was once enthusiastic about these cars, too.

About 20 years ago, CNN showcased an alternative-fuel vehicle
that I built with my own hands. I drove back and forth in front of the
camera, smiling from behind the wheel of my two-seater electric and
natural gas hybrid. I thought it was an especially beneficial solution
to our environmental challenges. I was wrong.

## Few Environmental Benefits

What counts as an alternative-energy vehicle and what doesn't is
hardly a straightforward reckoning. For instance, is an electric car a
true alternative if its drivetrain is ultimately powered by coal, nuclear
power, and lithium strip mines rather than petroleum? When the
Royal Society of Chemistry ran the numbers, it found that fully adopting electric cars in Britain would only reduce the country's $CO_2$ emissions by about 2 percent.

Electric vehicles don't eliminate the negative side effects of vehicular
travel. They simply move the problems elsewhere—often to contexts
where they become more opaque and difficult to address. When we
start to exchange one set of side effects for another, the exchange rates
become confusing. This opens a space for PR [public relations] firms,
news pundits, environmentalists, and others to step in and define the
terms of exchange to their liking.

## Cheap Fuel but Expensive Batteries

For instance, electric vehicle manufacturers claim that customers can fill up for ten cents per kilowatt-hour, which they say works out to pennies on the mile. But if buyers intend to drive their electric car beyond the length of the extension cord from their garage, they won't be able to take advantage of that cheap electricity. They'll have to rely on a battery—a battery they can only recharge a finite number of times before it must be replaced, at considerable expense.

The battery-construction step, not the "fuel" step, is the expensive part of driving an electric vehicle. Advanced batteries cost so much to fabricate that the ten-cent-per-kilowatt-hour "fuel" cost to charge them becomes negligible.

## The Oil Behind Electric Cars

Even though electric vehicles are moving to cheaper batteries, the costs of exhuming their required minerals extends far beyond simple

"How electric cars really work," cartoon by Jim Day, www.PoliticalCartoons.com. Copyright © 2011 by Jim Day and www.PoliticalCartoons.com. All rights reserved. Reproduced by permission.

dollars and cents. It takes a lot of fossil fuel to craft a battery. An analysis by the National Academies concludes that the environmental damage stemming from grid-dependent hybrids and electric vehicles will be greater than that of traditional gasoline-driven cars until at least 2030, even when assuming favorable technological advances. At current battery-production levels, mining activities already draw fire from local environmental and human rights organizations that are on the ground to witness the worst of the atrocities.

Even if mining companies clean up their operations (which at least will require much stricter international regulations) and engineers increase battery storage capacity (which they will, very slowly) there is still a bigger problem looming on the horizon: Alternative-fuel vehicles stand to define and spread patterns of "sustainable living" that cannot be easily sustained without cars.

## Perpetuating Sprawl and Waste

Cars enable people to spread out into patterns of suburban development, which induces ecological consequences beyond the side effects of the vehicle itself. Even the most efficient hybrid or electric cars can't resolve the larger ecological impacts of sprawl. In fact, their green badges of honor might even help them fuel it. For a time, this may not pose a problem, but eventually it will. Sprawl has positive and negative effects on Americans, but its intensification is clearly at odds with the long-term ideals of the environmental movement.

The suburban architecture of fully disengaged homes and megastores, connected by wide streets and highways, has prompted a mass deployment of energy resources that would have been unthinkable just a generation before its formation. It is from within the suburban addiction that Americans grew to understand extreme energy waste as perfectly normal.

This life isn't just wasteful. It's expensive, too. Relatively efficient city dwellers end up subsidizing new suburban road construction, power lines, sewers, and water mains—at a cost of about $13,426 per suburbanite, according to a recent study.

## Trading One Bad Habit for Another

Upon closer consideration, shifting from gasoline to electric vehicles starts to appear synonymous with switching a smoking habit from cloves to menthols. Even with all of the hype surrounding hybrid and electric vehicles, these machines are becoming somewhat of a cliché in some circles. Hybrid and electric vehicles may offer partial solutions within certain contexts, but those contexts are looking to be frightfully limited.

*Critics of electric cars say the battery technology required for such cars is expensive and can cost owners more in the long run than they would save on gasoline.*

It isn't acceptable for doctors to promote menthol cigarettes. Should environmentally minded people promote alternatively fueled automobiles? Some community groups are saying "No." They're showing how concerned citizens are better achieving their environmental objectives by supporting more durable options such as walkable neighborhoods, bicycling infrastructure, carpooling, traffic calming (incorporating physical features to slow or reduce traffic—wider sidewalks, roundabouts, etc.), and comfortable public transit.

These transportation strategies have a proven track record of success in cities across the globe. Beyond their greening impact, they can also make cities more vibrant, affordable, and pleasant places to live. Green strategies that improve people's lived experience, rather than emptying their wallets, have the potential to catch on.

Now that's genuinely energizing.

## EVALUATING THE AUTHOR'S ARGUMENTS:

Ozzie Zehner is a former supporter of electric and alternative-fuel vehicles—he even built one himself and promoted it before coming to the opinion that electric cars will never be as effective or cost-efficient as oil-fueled ones. Does knowing his background influence your opinion of his argument? Why or why not? Explain your reasoning.

# Facts About Oil

Editor's note: These facts can be used in reports to add credibility when making important points or claims.

## Facts About Global Oil Consumption

According to the US Energy Information Administration (EIA), the top fifteen oil-consuming nations (consumption of petroleum products and direct combustion of crude oil) in 2011 were:

1. United States: 18.8 million barrels of oil per day (bpd)
2. China: 9.8 million bpd
3. Japan: 4.5 million bpd
4. India: 3.3 million bpd
5. Russia: 3.1 million bpd
6. Saudi Arabia: 2.8 million bpd
7. Brazil: 2.6 million bpd
8. Germany: 2.4 million bpd
9. Canada: 2.2 million bpd
10. South Korea: 2.2 million bpd
11. Mexico: 2 million bpd
12. France: 1.8 million bpd
13. Iran: 1.7 million bpd
14. United Kingdom: 1.6 million bpd
15. Italy: 1.5 million bpd

The International Energy Agency reports the following about global oil consumption:

- 82.7 million bpd were consumed in 2009.
- 87.4 million bpd were consumed in 2010.
- 89.1 million bpd were consumed in 2011.
- 89.9 million bpd were forecast to be consumed in 2012.
- 90.9 million bpd are forecast to be consumed in 2013.

## Facts About Global Oil Production and Supply

According to the EIA, the top fifteen oil-product-producing nations (that is, producers of crude oil as well as natural gas and liquid fuel such as ethanol) as of 2011 were:

1. Saudi Arabia: 11.1 million bpd
2. Russia: 10.2 million bpd
3. United States: 10.1 million bpd
4. China: 4.3 million bpd
5. Iran: 4.2 million bpd
6. Canada: 3.7 million bpd
7. United Arab Emirates: 3.1 million bpd
8. Mexico: 3 million bpd
9. Kuwait: 2.7 million bpd
10. Brazil: 2.6 million bpd
11. Iraq: 2.6 million bpd
12. Nigeria: 2.5 million bpd
13. Venezuela: 2.5 million bpd
14. Norway: 2 million bpd
15. Algeria: 1.9 million bpd

According to the EIA, the top five crude oil–producing nations as of 2011 were:

1. Russia: 9.8 million bpd
2. Saudi Arabia: 9.5 million bpd
3. United States: 5.7 million bpd
4. China: 4.1 million bpd
5. Iran: 4.1 million bpd

According to the EIA, the top fifteen net oil importers (calculated by subtracting total oil production from consumption) in 2011 were:

1. United States: 8.7 million barrels per day
2. China: 5.5 million bpd
3. Japan: 4.3 million bpd
4. India: 2.3 million bpd
5. Germany: 2.3 million bpd
6. South Korea: 2.2 million bpd
7. France: 1.7 million bpd

8. Spain: 1.3 million bpd
9. Italy: 1.3 million bpd
10. Singapore: 1.2 million bpd
11. Taiwan: 1 million bpd
12. Netherlands: 944,000 bpd
13. Belgium: 637,000 bpd
14. Turkey: 623,000 bpd
15. Thailand: 592,000 bpd

According to the EIA, the top fifteen net oil exporters (calculated by subtracting consumption from total oil production) in 2011 were:

1. Saudi Arabia: 8.3 million bpd
2. Russia: 7.1 million bpd
3. Iran: 2.5 million bpd
4. United Arab Emirates: 2.5 million bpd
5. Kuwait: 2.3 million bpd
6. Nigeria: 2.3 million bpd
7. Iraq: 1.9 million bpd
8. Norway: 1.8 million bpd
9. Angola: 1.8 million bpd
10. Venezuela: 1.7 million bpd
11. Algeria: 1.6 million bpd
12. Qatar: 1.5 million bpd
13. Canada: 1.4 million bpd
14. Kazakhstan: 1.4 million bpd
15. Mexico: 881,000 bpd

According to the EIA and the *CIA World Factbook*, in 2012 the nations with the largest proven oil reserves were:

1. Saudi Arabia: 262.6 billion barrels
2. Venezuela: 211.2 billion barrels
3. Canada: 175.2 billion barrels
4. Iran: 137 billion barrels
5. Iraq: 115 billion barrels
6. Kuwait: 104 billion barrels
7. United Arab Emirates: 97.8 billion barrels
8. Russia: 60 billion barrels

9. Libya: 44.3 billion barrels
10. Nigeria: 37.2 billion barrels
11. Kazakhstan: 30 billion barrels
12. Qatar: 25.38 billion barrels
13. United States: 20.68 billion barrels
14. China: 14.8 billion barrels
15. Brazil: 12.86 billion barrels

Also according to the Energy Information Administration and the *CIA World Factbook:*

- Saudi Arabia has 17.85 percent of the world's total proven oil reserves.
- Venezuela has 14.35 percent of the world's total proven oil reserves.
- Canada has 11.91 percent of the world's total proven oil reserves.
- Iran has 9.31 percent of the world's total proven oil reserves.
- Iraq has 7.82 percent of the world's total proven oil reserves.
- Kuwait has 7.07 percent of the world's total proven oil reserves.
- The United Arab Emirates has 6.65 percent of the world's total proven oil reserves.
- Russia has 4.08 percent of the world's total proven oil reserves.
- Libya has 3.15 percent of the world's total proven oil reserves.
- Nigeria has 2.53 percent of the world's total proven oil reserves.
- Kazakhstan has 2.04 percent of the world's total proven oil reserves.
- Qatar has 1.72 percent of the world's total proven oil reserves.
- The United States has 1.41 percent of the world's total proven oil reserves.
- China has 1.01 percent of the world's total proven oil reserves.
- All other nations have less than 1 percent of the world's total proven oil reserves.

By region, that breaks down in the following way:

- The Middle East has 56 percent of the world's total proven oil reserves.
- North America has 16 percent of the world's total proven oil reserves.

- Africa has 9 percent of the world's total proven oil reserves.
- Central and South America have 8 percent of the world's total proven oil reserves.
- Asia and Oceania have 3 percent of the world's total proven oil reserves.
- Eurasia has 7 percent of the world's total proven oil reserves.
- Europe has 1 percent of the world's total proven oil reserves.

**Facts About Energy Use in the United States**
According to the EIA, as of 2011 the United States derived its total energy from the following sources (numbers total only 98 percent due to rounding):

| | |
|---|---|
| Petroleum/oil | 36 percent |
| Natural gas | 25 percent |
| Coal | 20 percent |
| Renewable energy | 9 percent |
| Nuclear energy | 8 percent |

Of the renewable energy sources that contributed to about 9 percent of the total US energy needs, the breakdown is as follows (numbers total only 99 percent due to rounding):

| | |
|---|---|
| Biomass | 48 percent |
| Hydroelectric | 35 percent |
| Wind | 13 percent |
| Geothermal | 2 percent |
| Solar | 1 percent |

By sector, energy consumption is as follows:

- The industrial sector of the economy consumed 31 percent of the total energy used in the United States.
- The transportation sector consumed 28 percent of the total energy used in the United States.
- The residential sector consumed 23 percent of the total energy used in the United States.
- The commercial sector consumed 19 percent of the total energy used in the United States.

## American Opinions About Oil

A 2012 Gallup poll asked Americans whether they thought protection of the environment should be given priority, even at the risk of limiting the amount of energy supplies such as oil, gas and coal, or whether development of US energy supplies such as oil, gas, and coal should be given priority, even if the environment suffers to some extent:

- Forty-four percent said the environment should be given priority.
- Forty-seven percent said energy should be given priority.
- Three percent said they should be given equal priority.
- Two percent said neither.
- One percent was unsure.

A 2012 Pew Research Center survey found:

- Sixty-five percent of Americans favor allowing more offshore oil and gas drilling in US waters.
- Thirty-one percent oppose such an action.
- Four percent were unsure.
- Sixty-nine percent favored increasing federal funding for research on wind, solar, and hydrogen technology.
- Twenty-six percent opposed such an action.
- Five percent were unsure.
- Forty-four percent favored promoting the increased use of nuclear power.
- Forty-nine percent opposed such an action.
- Seven percent were unsure.
- Forty-six percent favored giving tax cuts to energy companies to do more exploration for oil and gas.
- Fifty percent opposed such an action.
- Four percent were unsure.
- Seventy-eight percent favored requiring better fuel efficiency for cars, trucks, and SUVs.
- Nineteen percent opposed such an action.
- Three percent were unsure.
- Sixty-five percent favored spending more on subway, rail, and bus systems.
- Thirty-one percent opposed such an action.
- Four percent were unsure.

# Organizations to Contact

The editors have compiled the following list of organizations concerned with the issues debated in this book. The descriptions are derived from materials provided by the organizations. All have publications or information available for interested readers. The list was compiled on the date of publication of the present volume; the information provided here may change. Be aware that many organizations take several weeks or longer to respond to inquiries, so allow as much time as possible for the receipt of requested materials.

**Alternative Fuels Renewable Energies Council**
1029 Mumma Rd., Ste. 200
PO Box 185
Lemoyne, PA 17043
(717) 920-0528
website: www.afrec.net

The Alternative Fuels Renewable Energies Council promotes collaborations with industry to overcome technical, economic, and social barriers to commercial the use of alternative fuels.

**American Petroleum Institute (API)**
1220 L St. NW
Washington, DC 20005
(202) 682-8000
website: www.api.org

The API is a trade association representing America's petroleum industry. Its activities include lobbying, conducting research, and setting technical standards for the petroleum industry. The API publishes numerous position papers, reports, and information sheets, including some on the industry's response to oil spills and other oil-related current events.

**American Solar Energy Society (ASES)**
4760 Walnut St., Ste. 106
Boulder, CO 80301

(303) 443-3130
e-mail: ases@ases.org
website: www.ases.org

The ASES is the nation's leading association of solar professionals and advocates. The group's mission is to inspire an era of energy innovation and speed the transition to a sustainable energy economy.

**American Wind Energy Association (AWEA)**
1501 M St. NW, Ste. 1000
Washington, DC 20005
(202) 383-2500
e-mail: windmail@awea.org
website: www.awea.org

The AWEA represents wind power plant developers, wind turbine manufacturers, utilities, consultants, insurers, financiers, researchers, and others involved in the wind industry. The AWEA promotes the use of wind energy as a clean source of electricity for consumers around the world.

**Center for the Study of Carbon Dioxide and Global Change**
PO Box 25697
Tempe, AZ 85285-5697
(480) 966-3719
website: www.co2science.org

This nonprofit center is a project of three well-known global warming skeptics: geographer Craig D. Idso, botanist Keith E. Idso, and their physicist father, Sherwood B. Idso. The Idsos do not disclose their funding sources, but contributions to the center have been reported by ExxonMobil and the Western Fuels Association. Available on the website are numerous position papers, the weekly online newsletter $CO_2$ *Science*, and experiments/studies purporting to show that $CO_2$ benefits plants and plays no role in ocean acidification or atmospheric warming.

**Climate Change Division, US Environmental Protection Agency (EPA)**
Ariel Rios Bldg.
1200 Pennsylvania Ave. NW
Washington, DC 20460
(202) 272-0167
website: www.epa.gov/climatechange

The EPA is the federal agency in charge of protecting the environment and controlling pollution, mainly by issuing and enforcing regulations such as air quality and emissions standards, identifying and fining polluters, and cleaning up polluted sites. The agency's Climate Change Division's website is a well-organized source of climate-change indicators, scientific studies, explanations of federal greenhouse gas policy and regulatory initiatives, and FAQs for students and citizens.

### Electric Auto Association
847 Haight St.
San Francisco, CA 94117-3216
e-mail: contact@eaaev.org
website: www.eaaev.org

The Electric Auto Association promotes the widespread adoption of plug-in electric vehicles through education and advocacy. It publishes the newsletter *Current EVents*.

### Environmentally Conscious Consumers for Oil Shale
1055 Main St.
Grand Junction, CO 81501
(970) 241-3008
website: www.eccos.us

This nonprofit grassroots organization has members in Colorado, Utah, and Wyoming. Its goal is to educate the public on the vast potential and challenges of oil shale, including technology capable of extracting oil from shale, environmental concerns associated with oil shale, and socioeconomic issues related to oil shale use.

### Friends of the Earth
1025 Vermont Ave. NW, Ste. 300
Washington, DC 20005
(202) 783-7400
www.foe.org

Friends of the Earth is dedicated to protecting the planet from environmental disaster and preserving biological diversity. Toward this end, it supports energy policies that are environmentally and socially responsible.

**Global Wind Energy Council (GWEC)**
Wind Power House
80 Rue d'Arlon
1040 Brussels, Belgium
+32 2 213 1897
fax: +32 2 213 1890
website: www.gwec.net

The GWEC is the global wind industry trade association. The group's mission is to ensure that wind power establishes itself as one of the world's leading energy sources and provides substantial environmental and economic benefits.

**Greenpeace**
702 H St. NW, Ste. 300
Washington, DC 20001
(202) 462-1177
e-mail: info@wdc.greenpeace.org
website: www.greenpeace.org

Greenpeace is a nongovernment environmental activism organization that focuses on global issues, including energy use, alternative energy sources, and global warming. A multimedia library of photos, slideshows, and videos is also available on the website.

**Heartland Institute**
19 S. LaSalle St., Ste. 903
Chicago, IL 60603
(312) 377-4000
website: www.heartland.org

The institute is a nonprofit libertarian research and education organization. A vigorous opponent of government regulation of greenhouse gas emissions, it challenges the scientific consensus on global warming and sponsors and publishes research by global warming skeptics. Publications include books, videos, and a monthly newsletter.

**International Association for Hydrogen Energy (IAHE)**
5794 SW Fortieth St. #303
Miami, FL 33155
e-mail: info@iahe.org
website: www.iahe.org

The IAHE is a group of scientists and engineers professionally involved with the production and use of hydrogen. It hosts international forums to further its goal of creating an energy system based on hydrogen.

## International Panel on Climate Change (IPCC)
IPCC Secretariat
c/o World Meteorological Organization
7 bis Avenue de la Paix
C.P. 2300, CH-1211
Geneva 2, Switzerland
+41 22 730 8208
e-mail: ipcc-sec@wmo.int
website: www.ipcc.ch

The IPCC, created by the World Meteorological Organization and the United Nations Environment Programme in 1988, evaluates global climate change and the role of human activity in global warming, based on accumulated, international, scientific evidence and peer-reviewed, published findings. Recipient of the 2007 Nobel Peace Prize, the IPCC is widely cited as the world's foremost authority on the current status and likely effects of climate change. The *IPCC Fourth Assessment Report* (known as AR4), issued in 2007 and available in summary and full forms on the website, is an urgent call to action. In addition to the AR4, the IPCC publishes research papers on sea-level rise; updates on the *IPCC Fifth Assessment Report* (AR5), due in 2014; and a wide range of press releases, speeches, and graphs.

## National Biodiesel Board (NBB)
3337A Emerald Ln.
PO Box 104898
Jefferson City, MO 65110
(573) 635-3893
fax: (573) 635-7913
e-mail: info@biodiesel.org
website: www.biodiesel.org

The NBB represents the biodiesel industry and acts as the coordinating body for biodiesel research and development in the United States. The group's vision of the future is that by 2015 biodiesel will be viewed as an integral component of a national energy policy that increasingly relies on clean, domestic, renewable fuels.

**National Oil Shale Association (NOSA)**
PO Box 380
Glenwood Springs, CO 81602
(970) 389-0879
e-mail: natosa@comcast.net
website: www.oilshaleassoc.org

The NOSA was formed in the 1970s and was reinstated in 2007 in response to a resurgence of the oil shale industry. Its mission is to educate the public about oil shale in the United States and how extracting oil from shale can benefit the nation.

**National Renewable Energy Laboratory (NREL)**
1617 Cole Blvd.
Golden, CO 80401-3393
(303) 275-3000
website: www.nrel.gov

The NREL is the US Department of Energy's laboratory for renewable energy research, development, and deployment and a leading laboratory for energy efficiency. The laboratory's mission is to develop renewable energy and energy-efficiency technologies and practices, advance related science and engineering, and transfer knowledge and innovations to address the nation's energy and environmental goals.

**Nuclear Energy Institute (NEI)**
1776 I St. NW, Ste. 400
Washington, DC 20006-3708
(202) 739-8000
fax: (202) 785-4019
e-mail: webmasterp@nei.org
website: www.nei.org

The NEI is the policy organization of the nuclear energy industry. Its objective is to promote policies that benefit the nuclear energy business.

**Renewable Energy Policy Project (REPP)**
1612 K St. NW, Ste. 202
Washington, DC 20006
(202) 293-2898
fax: (202) 298-5857

e-mail: info2@repp.org
website: www.repp.org

The REPP provides information about solar, hydrogen, biomass, wind, hydrogen, and other forms of renewable energy.

## Renewable Fuels Association (RFA)
425 Third St. SW, Ste. 1150
Washington, DC 20024
(202) 289-3835
e-mail: info@ethanolrfa.org
website: www.ethanolrfa.org

The RFA is made up of professionals who research, produce, and market renewable fuels, especially alcohol-based fuels like ethanol.

## Sierra Club
85 Second St., 2nd Fl.
San Francisco, CA 94105
(415) 977-5500
fax: (415) 977-5799
e-mail: info@sierraclub.org
website: www.sierraclub.org

The Sierra Club is a grassroots environmental organization that works to protect communities, wild places, and the planet itself. It favors the use of alternative energy sources. Its website features news articles, links to several different blogs, an e-mail newsletter, and information about both local and international outings.

## Union of Concerned Scientists (UCS)
2 Brattle Sq.
Cambridge, MA 02238-9105
(617) 547-5552
website: www.ucsusa.org

The UCS works to advance responsible public policy in areas where science and technology play a vital role. Its programs focus on safe and renewable energy technologies, transportation reform, arms control, and sustainable agriculture. UCS publications include the quarterly magazine *Nucleus*, the briefing papers *Motor-Vehicle Fuel Efficiency and Global Warming* and *Global Environmental Problems: A Status Report*, and the book *Cool Energy: The Renewable Solution to Global Warming*.

**US Environmental Protection Agency (EPA)**
Ariel Rios Bldg.
1200 Pennsylvania Ave. NW
Washington, DC 20460
(202) 272-0167
website: www.epa.gov

The EPA's mission is to protect human health and the environment. Its website features news releases, research topics, information on laws and regulations, a "Science and Technology" section, and a search engine that brings up a wide variety of articles related to energy and the environment.

# For Further Reading

## Books

Cooper, Andrew Scott. *The Oil Kings: How the U.S., Iran, and Saudi Arabia Changed the Balance of Power in the Middle East.* New York: Simon & Schuster, 2011. Explores how oil came to dominate US domestic and international affairs.

Heinberg, Richard. *Peak Everything: Waking Up to the Century of Declines.* Gabriola Island, BC: New Society, 2010. Discusses how explosive growth in the twentieth century ushered in an era of declines, including a decline in oil and other fossil fuels.

Klare, Michael T. *The Race for What's Left: The Global Scramble for the World's Last Resources.* New York: Metropolitan, 2012. An expert on natural resource issues argues that the world is facing an unprecedented crisis of resource depletion—a crisis that goes beyond "peak oil" to encompass shortages of coal, uranium, copper, lithium, water, and arable land.

Maass, Peter. *Crude World: The Violent Twilight of Oil.* New York: Knopf, 2009. Explores oil's impact on the countries that produce it.

Yergin, Daniel. *The Quest: Energy, Security, and the Remaking of the Modern World.* New York: Penguin, 2011. This book, by a renowned energy expert, offers a gripping account of the global quest for energy.

## Periodicals and Internet Sources

Adams, O.R., Jr. "New Evidence That Man-Made Carbon Dioxide ($CO_2$) Does Not Cause Global Warming," *American Traditions Magazine*, 2011. www.americantraditions.org/Articles/New%20 Evidence%20that%20Man-Made%20Carbon%20Dioxide%20 (CO2)%20Does%20Not%20Cause%20Global%20Warming.htm.

Ambrose, Jay. "Fracking Not a Public Health Threat," *News-Herald* (Ohio), August 20, 2011. www.news-herald.com/articles /2011/08/20/opinion/nh4391316.txt?viewmode=fullstory.

Bateman, Christopher. "A Colossal Fracking Mess," *Vanity Fair*, June 21, 2010. www.vanityfair.com/business/features/2010/06/fracking -in-pennsylvania-201006.

Black, Edwin. "When the Pump Runs Dry," *Baltimore Sun*, February 27, 2012. http://articles.baltimoresun.com/2012-02-27/news/bs-ed-oil-interruption-20120227_1_crude-abqaiq-international-energy-agency.

Borenstein, Severin. "Making the Wrong Case for Renewable Energy," Bloomberg News Service, February 14, 2012. www.bloomberg.com/news/2012-02-14/making-wrong-case-for-renewable-energy-commentary-by-severin-borenstein.html.

Bryce, Robert. "The Oil Shocks and the Costly Delusion of Energy 'Independence,'" *Viewpoints* special edition: *The 1979 'Oil Shock:' Legacy, Lessons, and Lasting Reverberations*, Middle East Institute, 2009. www.voltairenet.org/IMG/pdf/1979_OIl_Shock.pdf.

Cantarow, Ellen. "Shale-Shocked," *Huffington Post*, January 23, 2012. www.huffingtonpost.com/ellen-cantarow/marcellus-shale-fracking_b_1223903.html?ref=green.

Committee on America's Climate Choices. *America's Climate Choices*, National Research Council, May 2011. www.nap.edu/catalog.php?record_id=12781.

Energy Policy Research Foundation. *The Bakken Boom: An Introduction to North Dakota's Shale Oil*, August 3, 2011. www.eprinc.org/pdf/EPRINC-BakkenBoom.pdf.

Fischetti, Mark. "Can We Get Off Oil Now?," *Observations* (blog), *Scientific American*, February 28, 2011. http://blogs.scientificamerican.com/observations/2011/02/28/can-we-get-off-oil-now.

Flintoff, Corey. "Where Does America Get Oil? You May Be Surprised," National Public Radio, April 12, 2012. www.npr.org/2012/04/11/150444802/where-does-america-get-oil-you-may-be-surprised.

Food & Water Watch. "The Case for a Ban on Gas Fracking," June 2011. http://documents.foodandwaterwatch.org/doc/frackingReport.pdf.

Frederick, Sherman. "The Lies We Tell About Green Energy," *Las Vegas Review Journal*, September 4, 2011. www.lvrj.com/opinion/the-lies-we-tell-about-green-energy-129208378.html.

Green, Kenneth P. "Electric Cars: Doubling Down on Dumb," American Enterprise Institute, February 1, 2012. www.aei.org

/article/energy-and-the-environment/electric-cars-doubling-down
-on-dumb.

Hansen, James. "Game Over for the Climate," *New York Times*, May
10, 2012. www.nytimes.com/2012/05/10/opinion/game-over-for
-the-climate.html.

Helm, Dieter. "Look to Gas for the Future," *Prospect*, March 25,
2011. www.prospectmagazine.co.uk/magazine/peak-oil-energy
-future-gas.

Jamail, Dahr. "The Scourge of 'Peak Oil,'" Al Jazeera, July 25, 2011. www
.aljazeera.com/indepth/features/2011/07/201172081613634207
.html.

Jerving, Sara. "The Fracking Frenzy's Impact on Women," Center
for Media and Democracy, April 4, 2012. www.prwatch.org
/news/2012/04/11204/fracking-frenzys-impact-women.

Kimron, Shlomit. "What Happens in 50 Years When the Oil
Runs Out?," *Haaretz*, August 18, 2010. www.haaretz.com/print
-edition/business/what-happens-in-50-years-when-the-oil-runs
-out-1.308685.

King, David, and James Murray. "Oil's Tipping Point Has Passed,"
*Nature*, January 26, 2012.

Klare, Michael T. "What Will Replace Oil?," *Salon*, June 27, 2011.
www.salon.com/2011/06/27/energy_future.

Krauss, Clifford. "New Technologies Redraw the World's Energy
Picture," *New York Times*, October 25, 2011. www.nytimes
.com/2011/10/26/business/energy-environment/new-technologies
-redraw-the-worlds-energy-picture.html?pagewanted=all.

Lane, Charles. "Electric Cars and Liberals' Refusal to Accept Science,"
*Washington Post*, March 5, 2012. www.washingtonpost.com/opin
ions/electric-cars-and-the-liberal-war-with-science/2012/03/05
/gIQA7SpYtR_story.html.

LeVine, Steve. "Can the Electric Car Survive?," *Slate*, March 13,
2012. www.slate.com/articles/technology/future_tense/2012/03
/chevy_volt_nissan_leaf_will_the_electric_car_ever_be_a_success_
.html.

Lynch, Michael C. "The Case Against Fracking Is Anecdotal and
Overstated," *U.S. News & World Report*, February 21, 2012.
www.usnews.com/opinion/blogs/on-energy/2012/02/21/the-case
-against-fracking-is-anecdotal-and-misleading.

Lynch, Michael C. "'Peak Oil' Is a Waste of Energy," *New York Times*, August 25, 2009. www.nytimes.com/2009/08/25/opinion/25lynch .html?pagewanted=1.

Mannle, Andy. "Is Nuclear Energy a Fuel with a Future?," *World Energy Monitor*, October 2011.

Motavalli, Jim. "For the Electric Car, a Slow Road to Success," *Yale Environment 360*, January 26, 2012. http://e360.yale.edu/feature /for_the_electric_car_a_slow_road_to_success/2488.

Nocera, Joe. "How to Frack Responsibly," *New York Times*, February 28, 2012. www.nytimes.com/2012/02/28/opinion/nocera-how-to -frack-responsibly.html.

Noel, Michael D. "The Promise of Unconventional Oil," *Oil & Gas Journal*, December 19, 2011. www.oilgasmonitor.com/promise -unconventional-oil/1068.

Powers, Jonathan. "Oil Addiction: Fueling Our Enemies," Truman National Security Project, February 17, 2010. www.trumanproject .org/files/papers/Oil_Addiction_-_Fueling_Our_Enemies_FINAL .pdf.

Rubin, Jeff. "We Have Run Out of Oil We Can Afford to Burn," *Globe and Mail* (Toronto), October 6, 2010. www.theglobeandmail .com/report-on-business/commentary/jeff-rubins-smaller-world/we -have-run-out-of-oil-we-can-afford-to-burn/article1743497.

*Washington Times*. "Unplug the Volt," January 17, 2012. www.wash ingtontimes.com/news/2012/jan/17/unplug-the-volt.

Weinstein, Amanda L., and Mark D. Partridge. "The Economic Value of Shale Natural Gas in Ohio," Ohio State University, December 2011. http://aede.osu.edu/sites/drupal-aede.web/files /Economic%20Value%20of%20Shale%20Dec%202011.pdf.

Yergin, Daniel. "Oil's New World Order," *Washington Post*, October 18, 2011. www.washingtonpost.com/opinions/daniel -yergin-for-the-future-of-oil-look-to-the-americas-not-the-middle -east/2011/10/18/gIQAxdDw7L_story.html.

———. "What's Behind Rising Gas Prices?," *Wall Street Journal*, March 25, 2012. http://online.wsj.com/article/SB100014240527 02304459804577281580476174366.html.

Young, Gregory. "CO$_2$ Fairytales in Global Warming," *American Thinker*, January 11, 2009. www.americanthinker.com/2009/01/co2_fairytales_in_global_warmi.html.

Zerbe, L. "5 Facts About Fracking Every Family Needs to Know," *Rodale News*. www.rodale.com/fracking-2.

Zuckerman, Mortimer. "With Fracking America Can Escape the Energy Trap," *U.S. News & World Report*, December 2, 2011. www.usnews.com/opinion/articles/2011/12/02/zuckerman-with-fracking-american-can-escape-the-energy-trap.

## Websites

**Coming Global Oil Crisis** (www.oilcrisis.com). This site considers what a post-oil world might look like.

**Energy Bulletin.net** (www.energybulletin.net). This site, maintained by the Post Carbon Institute, offers breaking and regional news related to the topic of oil.

**Go Beyond Oil** (www.gobeyondoil.org). This site, maintained by the environmental group Greenpeace, urges the world to find an alternative energy source, and fast.

**National Commission on the BP *Deepwater Horizon* Oil Spill and Offshore Drilling** (www.oilspillcommission.gov). This website was set up after the catastrophic oil spill in the Gulf of Mexico in 2010. Maintained by the formal commission appointed to examine the causes and ramifications of the spill, it offers information about the spill and shares the commission's recommendations on how to proceed with deepwater drilling.

**Oil Drum** (www.theoildrum.com). This website considers many topics related to the future of energy. Archived articles, blog posts, and conversations inform readers on many aspects of the energy debate.

**Oil, US Department of Energy** (http://energy.gov/oil). This site, maintained by the US Department of Energy, offers numerous charts, graphs, fact sheets, and other statistical information pertaining to US oil use.

**Peak Oil Crisis** (www.peak-oil-crisis.com). This site features an oil consumption counter that calculates how many barrels of oil have been consumed to date.

**RealClimate** (www.realclimate.org). This website features commentary from climate scientists on the topics related to climate change, including oil and energy.

# Index

N

National Bureau of Economic Research, 85

*National Geographic* (magazine), 40

National Park Service, 105

National Renewable Energy Laboratory, 92

Natural gas
  extraction from shale, *33*
  global reserves of, *31*
  growth in US production of, 65
  projected US production of, *31*
  from shale, 30, 32

New York Mercantile Exchange, 61

*New York Times* (newspaper), 104

Nuclear energy
  can replace oil, 77–83
  costs of, 96–97
  is not good alternative to oil, 84–90

Nuclear Energy Institute, 80

Nuclear power plants, *79, 89*
  numbers of/percentage of electricity produced by, 80

O

Obama, Barack, 18, 20, 100, 104, 111
  on drilling to solve energy problem, 41

Off-shore drilling, 8, 55
  number of exploration rigs for, 46

Oil
  anniversary of, should be celebrated, 44–48
  current global demand for, 12
  discovery of, 45
  global reserves of, *31*
  is finite resource, 11–16
  is problematic resource, 37–43
  is renewable resource, 17–21
  national security is not undermined by use of, 57–63
  national security is undermined by use of, 49–56
  nuclear energy can replace, 77–83
  nuclear energy is not good alternative to, 84–90
  price of, 116
  products derived from, *24, 47*
  projected consumption of, *42*
  projected decline in supplies of, *15, 26*
  projected growth in supply of, by country, *68*
  renewable resources can replace, 91–98
  renewable resources cannot replace, 99–106
  society will break down from depletion of, 22–27
  world will never have to make do without, 28–35

# Picture Credits

© AP Images, 74

© AP Images/Gerald Herbert, 36

© artpartner-images/Alamy, 13

© Martyn F. Chillmaid/Photo Researchers, Inc., 24

© Chad Ehlers/Alamy, 79

© Gale/Cengage Learning, 15, 26, 31, 42, 47, 51, 62, 68, 81, 87, 97, 103, 109

© Peter Horree/Alamy, 89

© Doug Houghton/Alamy, 10

© Hulton Archive/Illustrated London News/Getty Images, 45

© INTERFOTO/Alamy, 19

© Ingo Jezierski/Alamy, 117

© Wang Jianwei/Xinhua/Landov, 39

© Patti McConville/Alamy, 67

© Prisma Bildagentur AG/Alamy, 76

© Jim Lo Scalzo/EPA/Landov, 54

© Jochen Tack/Alamy, 94, 104

© Mario Tama/Getty Images, 61

© Terry Smith Images/Alamy, 33

© ZUMA Wire Service/Alamy, 111